MIDWEST  REFLECTIONS

Memoirs and personal histories of the people of the Upper Midwest

EGGS IN THE COFFEE, SHEEP IN THE CORN
My 17 Years as a Farm Wife
Marjorie Myers Douglas

DANCING THE COWS HOME
A Wisconsin Girlhood
Sara De Luca

HALFWAY HOME
A Granddaughter's Biography
Mary Logue

FROM THE HIDEWOOD
Memories of a Dakota Neighborhood
Robert Amerson

Barefoot on Crane Island

Me, about 1916

Barefoot on
Crane Island

For Alice & Hallie

MARJORIE MYERS DOUGLAS

Marjorie Myers Douglas
9-20-98

MINNESOTA HISTORICAL SOCIETY PRESS · ST. PAUL

MIDWEST REFLECTIONS
Memoirs and personal histories of the people of the Upper Midwest

Published with funds provided to the Minnesota Historical Society by the Elmer L. and Eleanor J. Andersen Publications Endowment Fund.

Manufactured in the United States of America
10 9 8 7 6 5 4 3 2 1

International Standard Book Number
0-87351-362-2 (cloth)   0-87351-363-0 (paper)

♾ The paper used in this publication meets the minimum requirements of the American National Standard for Information Sciences—Permanence for Printed Library Materials, ANSI Z39.48-1984.

Library of Congress Cataloging-in-Publication Data
Douglas, Marjorie M.
    Barefoot on Crane Island / Marjorie Myers Douglas.
        p.   cm.   — (Midwest Reflections)
    ISBN 0-87351-362-2 (cloth : alk. paper). — ISBN 0-87351-363-0 (pbk. : alk. paper)
    1. Crane Island (Minn.)—Social life and customs. 2. Crane Island (Minn.)—Biography. 3. Crane Island (Minn.)—History. 4. Douglas, Marjorie M.—Childhood and youth. I. Title. II. Series.
    F612.H5D68   1998
    977.6'77—dc21   98-15457
                                                                            CIP

Photograph of the *Hopkins* is from the Minnesota Historical Society collections; all other photographs are from the collection of the author.

To My Husband
Donald Moats Douglas
with whom I shared almost
fifty-two years of marriage
I dedicate this memoir of the
childhood summers
before I knew him

Contents

Preface   xi

Wildlife   3
A Haircut, Herons, and History   16
Three Times of Danger   32
Blackie   45
Painful Parting, Joyous Reunion   55
Living Legends   71
Pirates   85
Dance of the Raccoons and Dance
    of the Heavens   100
Raindrops and Teardrops   113
"Socks," My Modest Brother   120
Swim!   133
Unsinkable Crane Island   147
Ev, the Family Rascal   156
Superdad   169
Ambivalence   184
I Find Out about Boys   191
A Swain Is Tested   201
The Real World   211
My Friend the Loon   219

Afterword   224

Preface

CRANE ISLAND is a tiny scrap of land in the remote western end of Lake Minnetonka's Upper Lake, all but forgotten among the beauties of the lake's three hundred miles of irregular wooded shoreline and unexpected bays, islands, and peninsulas. It lies a few watery miles from the town of Excelsior, Minnesota, and about twenty-five miles west of Minneapolis, where my father taught German at the University of Minnesota. My family spent summers there from 1917, when I was five, until my older brother, Bob, and I had finished college, and my younger brother, Everett, had married and moved away. Dad and Mother continued to enjoy the cottage until after Mother's death in 1952, and then it was sold.

The island had been a heronry until 1906, when a storm swept all the trees from its center and the birds moved to the neighboring island of Wawatasso. A group from Bethlehem Presbyterian Church then bought the property, formed the Crane Island Association, and surveyed lots around the periphery, where cottages were built all facing the lake. They put up a caretaker's lodge, an icehouse, and a tennis court in the center of what was known as the Commons. As in a New England community, where all the neighboring farmers used common grazing land, we all freely enjoyed the Commons.

My first book, *Eggs in the Coffee, Sheep in the Corn: My 17 Years as a Farm Wife,* was published in 1994 by the Minnesota Historical Society Press. Working on it stirred many powerful memories of my youth and the island, and I began to write them down (changing some names and minor details to protect the privacy of others). My memories of Crane Island are of idyllic, timeless, untroubled summer days, filled with the small challenges and victories of youth and the love of my parents.

My mother, Olinia May Mattison Myers, was born July 5, 1878, one of seven children of a scholarly Methodist minister and his saintly wife; she proudly traced her English ancestry back to the American colonists. She was barely five feet tall, but her honest, nearsighted blue eyes shone confident, steady, and unperturbed by life's minor problems. After graduation from Northwestern University, where, loyal to her parents' expectations, she distinguished herself as a student, she worked as a librarian.

There she also met my father, Walter Raleigh Myers. He too wore a Phi Beta Kappa key and was almost entirely of English ancestry. He was also born in July, on the ninth, but in 1881. His father was a carpenter, a Civil War veteran who lived his religion in his every act. After my parents married, they traveled to Germany, where my father prepared for his doctorate in German language and they made many friends. Dad's previous study trip abroad had been as a hired hand on a cattle boat, for he had to finance his education by his own efforts. He was tall — five feet, ten inches — and wore his brown hair in a pompadour so that, with his erect carriage, he looked even taller. He combined an idealistic outlook toward people with many practical skills and an eagerness for learning and adventure.

As I wrote about my parents, I found it difficult to portray my beloved mother. But as I pondered and discussed our childhood with my brothers, I gained insight into her poised, practical, loving ways; she was the balance wheel for all the family. I have come to believe that she and I were so loving and close that I could not "see" her. My enthusiasms, my concerns, my joys echoed those of my father, whom I idolized.

I was able to supplement my memories of the island with research. In 1990 an extended study of Crane Island's unusual history was undertaken; as a result of the study, the island was placed on the National Register of Historic Places as the Crane Island Historic District in 1991. This material was made available to me through the kindness of Dr. Robert A. Larsen, an initiator of the request for designation and owner of what I knew as the Dickson cottage. It delights me to know that the island's peaceful isolation and precious privacy are still protected and preserved.

I also used the detailed minutes of the Crane Island Association, held in the capacious files of the Minnesota Historical Society. This material has been invaluable in my presentation of the island's history.

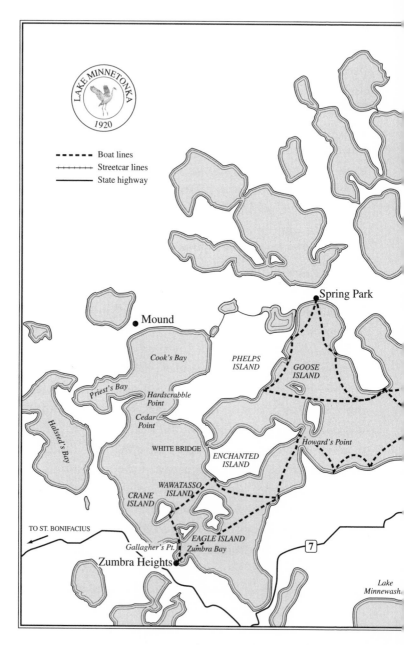

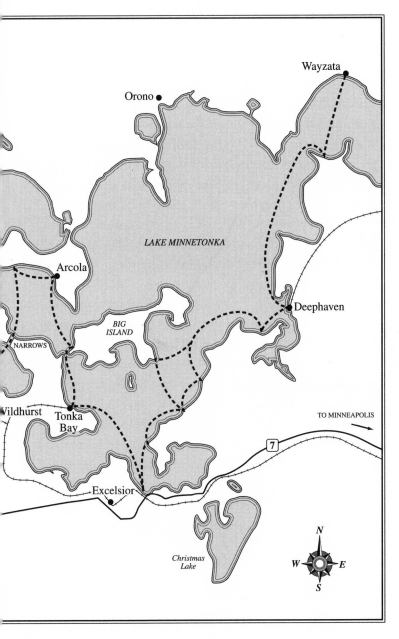

Margot Fortunato Galt, Ann Regan, Sally Rubinstein, and Lynn Marasco have provided much-appreciated guidance and editing. My brothers and my friends have contributed their memories and explained their deductions. Pat and Zola and Mary and the ladies from Lynnhurst have read and discussed portions of the manuscript. Kit Ketchum and my sons are again the angels of my computer. All have greatly added to my enjoyment in the sometimes surprisingly moving experience of remembering and writing.

Soon after I began to record these memories, a group of volunteers from the Minnesota Transportation Museum, led by Leo Maloche and evidently as nostalgic as I about Lake Minnetonka's early days, finished restoring the steamboat *Minnehaha,* one of the famous "Yellow Fleet" that once met the streetcars at Excelsior and provided transportation to twenty-seven stops around the lake, the most remote of which was Crane Island. These boats made possible our summers on the island. When cars became common and people began to rely on their own boats, three streetcar boats were consigned to a watery grave in 1926; two more followed soon after. The last of them, the *Hopkins,* was scuttled in 1949. The *Minnehaha,* now recovered and lovingly restored, once again plies the lake, offering a taste of an earlier era and making new memories for those who love Minnesota summers at the lake.

Barefoot on Crane Island

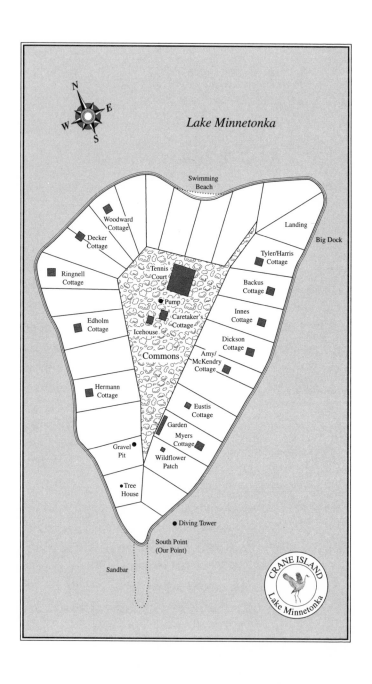

Lake Minnetonka

Swimming Beach

Woodward Cottage

Decker Cottage

Landing

Big Dock

Ringnell Cottage

Tennis Court

Tyler/Harris Cottage

Backus Cottage

Pump

Innes Cottage

Edholm Cottage

Caretaker's Cottage

Icehouse

Dickson Cottage

Commons

Amy/ McKendry Cottage

Hermann Cottage

Eustis Cottage

Garden

Gravel Pit

Myers Cottage

Wildflower Patch

Tree House

Diving Tower

South Point (Our Point)

Sandbar

CRANE ISLAND
Lake Minnetonka

Wildlife

DAD LIFTED ME out of the rowboat and onto the dock that bright morning in the spring of 1918, and I scrambled up the steep wooden stairs to the foot of the lawn. Deaf to the shrill shouts of my two brothers and barely glancing up the slope to the cottage, I sat down on the grass, took off my shoes and stockings, and wriggled my toes, freed for my first day of going barefoot. At last the cottage on Crane Island in Lake Minnetonka was really ours and not just rented.

That meant the wildflower patch I had dreamed about all winter was now mine! In my haste to reach it, I forgot how twigs and stones in the grass could prick and stab. Flinching a bit at each step, I hurried to the circular area beyond the trees where the tall swing would soon hang. There Dutchman's-breeches grew in profusion. They were so like bleeding hearts except for their delicate coral color. Joy of joys: they were in bloom!

I surveyed the wildflowers and took a deep breath. My very own garden. Last summer, when I was five, I had learned to pull the weeds, keeping a careful watch for the nettles that could sting and raise burning streaks on my flesh. This year, I promised myself, I'd not allow a single weed.

I knelt to pick a bouquet and was startled to find a large spiderweb, its gossamer filaments suspended in an intricate pattern from the leaves. The sun touched drops of dew caught in the web and sparkled there. I marveled that Miss Muffet's frightening companion could produce this creation as filmy as fairy wings. I felt a rush of love for that clever spider.

Without disturbing the web, I picked one after another of the graceful fronds. I examined one bloom closely. It was, indeed, in the shape of bulging fat man's pants. The leaves were lacy like the maidenhair fern, and I picked enough to edge my bouquet, carefully rotating it in my fist to keep it balanced.

I started to the cottage for a vase, then saw my mother in a long khaki skirt and white blouse proceeding steadily up the slope. Mother typically stood very straight, as if stretching to be taller, but now she was hunched over an armful of packages. I was filled with remorse, for I had not carried anything. I ran to show her my flowers and ask to help.

Mother paused and smiled indulgently, "Yes, thank you, Marjorie. Catch this umbrella that's slipping out from under my arm, will you? And you may help Daddy when he's ready to get water and give your flowers a drink."

My nine-year-old brother Bob was efficiently pulling a tarpaulin from the canoe, which filled every inch of space on the front porch overlooking the lake. So we had to walk around the cottage to the kitchen door. From the kitchen the yard sloped gradually in every direction but one. A level path along the north fence led west past a narrow building divided into outhouse, workshop, and firewood shed and beyond that the vegetable garden.

Suddenly we heard Everett's high-pitched voice yelling, "I've caught one! I've caught one! Where shall I plant him?"

My four-year-old brother clutched a tiny, brown field mouse that was squeaking and thrashing its paws. Fortunately, he had caught it by the back of the neck so it could not bite him. Evidently he remembered last summer when our father buried field mice killed in the traps, and now he was trying to help by offering to "plant" this one. Dad dropped the suitcases he was carrying and, in long strides, reached his little boy. He killed the mouse and set it aside for future burial. I was grateful not to be part of that. I was sure those little creatures had families just as Peter Rabbit did. They would be missed at home.

This morning we three children had waited at "608," our big house in Minneapolis, watching out the bay window that faced a little triangular park on the Mississippi River, while our parents collected the last of our baggage. We could not come back till fall because Dad had rented the house fully furnished at forty dollars a month for the summer. But that didn't matter. Now we owned our Crane

Island cottage. For a little over a thousand dollars Dad had bought it. All five of us were excited.

This year we had a plan — really it was Mother's plan. We were to pull the faded building paper off the walls in the L-shaped living-dining room. The paper, thick and soft as felt, had provided insulation for an older couple who had once lived all winter in our cottage, heated only by a little wood-burning potbellied stove, which had an isinglass peephole in its door, that also served them as a cookstove. (A kitchen had been added later.)

The blue building paper, which had been tacked to the wall studs, had faded unevenly and in places turned brownish. Mother said it was hideous. We kids were eager when on Saturday morning she tied a towel over her hair and proclaimed, "This is the day."

Dad, garbed in a carpenter's apron, was equipped with great heavy shears with long, hungry-looking blades and wooden handles. He always seemed to know how to do everything. Some of the paper tore off in sheets, some in small pieces, but gradually the two-by-fours appeared, and the room began to turn a warm brown instead of streaked blue.

Bob and I had been carrying the discarded scraps to the clothes basket as Dad ripped them off when my brother suddenly hollered at me, "Drop that, Marj."

I was so surprised that I let go of the pie-sized piece of building paper I had been carrying. As it struck the floor with a soft thud, a spider was jarred loose — a large spider with a furry body and short legs. It moved slowly, lazily, until it was hidden again under the edge of the paper.

"What is it, Bob?" Dad inquired a little impatiently. But Mother had seen and quickly beckoned both of us children across the room to where Ev was constructing a boat with his blocks.

I don't think even Dad had ever seen such a huge spider. Its body looked as big as the yolk of the coddled egg I'd had for breakfast. It clung to the cardboard, accustomed, I suppose, to being unmolested in its dark hideaway in the wall. Dad carried it outside, where he "squished it," he told us. All I could think of was how glad I was that Bob had noticed it before it bit me and that it was gone.

A horrid thought suddenly struck me. I remembered the diaphanous web in my garden and my feeling of kinship with a creature that could create anything so beautiful. Now, seeing the reality of a live spider's ugliness, I was filled with loathing. And I was ashamed of my disloyalty.

"Was that the kind that bites, Daddy?" I asked, still looking in awe at my hand, which had been so close to terrible danger.

"They all bite, Marjorie, and this one was big enough to have quite a bit of poison in his body."

"I saw one in the woodshed," Bob said, "but it had a tiny body and skinny legs and ran away from me."

"A daddy longlegs, maybe," Dad guessed, but Mother added soberly, "You'd better leave spiders to your father, Robert, until you learn to tell the difference."

"I didn't like this bad spider one bit," I piped up, looking at the walls yet to be uncovered and still feeling disloyal. "Are there any more in there? Spiders should stay outdoors." I pouted a little.

"There's one, Daddy!" Everett, curious about the to-do, pointed an accusing finger at the ceiling, where, sure enough, another fat, scary spider was slowly crawling.

"Right you are! We'll see about that big fellow." Turning to my mother, he said, "Why don't you and the children go for a swim, and I'll have another look around here."

Dad's taking charge was the end of the worry for me — until evening, that is. Then I hesitated to go into the bedroom where I slept alone, so he brought the boys along and all of us piled onto my bed for a good-night story. Bob was still dressed in his knickers, worn thin at the knees, but Ev and I liked the gray and tan shorts Mother stitched up on her sewing machine. Actually, none of us paid much attention to what we wore on Crane Island.

Looking out at the living room, I began to think about the couple who had lived there all one winter.

"Did that little stove really keep the Joneses warm when it snowed, Daddy? And weren't they awfully lonesome?"

I cuddled comfortably against him as he replied, "But Mr. Jones had been sick and needed to be quiet, so this was a good place for him, wasn't it?"

"What about when the ice was breaking up in the spring?" Bob asked. He always wanted to figure things out. "How did they cross the ice to get milk and stuff?"

Dad did his usual trick of making us try to find the answer ourselves. With the help of many hints, we finally guessed that the Joneses had pushed a light boat ahead of them on the ice until a crack broke open, then jumped into the boat. It sounded dangerous. Bob wasn't satisfied and puzzled long over the problem. We pictured them with snow drifted high against the doors. A piano and an old treadle sewing machine came with the cottage. Perhaps these helped them pass the time when they wearied of the collection of records for the wind-up phonograph.

Our talk temporarily dispelled my concerns about the spiders. I loved that little downstairs bedroom, which Dad and Mother and I used for a dressing room. To put myself to sleep, I lay on my back and looked upward out the window where the trees framed a circle of sky. Even if there was no moon I could usually see bats play there, making a crisscross pattern with their swift, dipping flight.

When the walls were finally all uncovered and cleaned, Mother let us hang some pictures from our storybooks between the uprights, and that was decoration enough. We ate and played on the front porch, and my parents slept there. No more spiders appeared until weeks afterward, when Mother and I found one crawling along the bedroom floor in the corner where we had put our tennis shoes. I began to dream of great webs so beautiful I reached out to climb them to marvelous adventures only to have a great menacing spider break through and spring at me. So Dad found a book at the Minneapolis Public Library — where he had once taken us to see curator Grace Wiley and her collection of snakes — that told about different kinds of spiders and their habits. After that we expected to encounter them occasionally in the tool shop or in the storage space under the house where we sometimes played "explorers," but then we were invading their territory, so we tried to keep a respectful distance.

We children were more curious about than afraid of wildlife. I remember no squeamishness about hunting or picking up the "thousand-leggeds" we found on the island and saved at two cents apiece for Dad's friend Dr. Sigerfoos, who taught zoology at the university. All three of us took on the assignment enthusiastically, aware that great fortune would be ours. In the winter our allowances were just the "Saturday pennies" we carried to the corner grocery store, where we made the excruciating decision between three-for-a-penny licorice and four-for-a-penny peppermints.

The ten-acre island was a rough triangle. The North End, with its Big Dock and its swimming beach cut out of the reeds, was rounded, as was the bulge on the west. The South Point, which we called Our Point, was a sandy finger reaching far out toward the mainland from the low

My brothers and me on our dock at Crane Island

tangle of shrubbery and birch and aspen trees south of our cottage. Dr. Lillehei's home was later built below the bluff at the foot of our sloping lawn, but in the Myers heyday the whole point was treated as ours, including the plateau by the gravel pit, the main swimming beach (twenty feet deep on the east side, a gradual descent on the west), and my wildflower patch in the hollow. Dad kept it up for everyone to use.

As soon as we were settled in, Dad found time for fishing and one day snagged a giant turtle by the flipper. He managed to get the foot-and-a-half-long creature into the boat and carried it to the dooryard to show to us. He called it a "leatherback" and pointed out the brown decorations on its peaked, greenish-yellow shell, more pliable than those of the common painted-shell turtles. Its disposition was gentler—much gentler—than that of the snapping turtles we had learned to avoid. It was too big to fit into a bucket, so Dad sent Bob for the laundry tub. Before he got back, the animal stuck out its long neck with a slender head and pencil-thin nose and began to scramble across the grass. Unafraid, Everett at once begged for a ride, and Dad held him steady on the turtle's slippery back for a lurching trip around the yard. By the time Bob and I each had a turn, the turtle was slowing down, and Dad, to my consternation, began talking of soup. Feeling confused, I kept my concerns to myself, accepted my father's wisdom, and didn't "make a fuss," which I had learned was unwelcome in our family.

After Dad got his ax from the toolshed, the turtle refused to stick its neck out. We waited. We talked in whispers. We stayed out of its range of vision. We waited. Long after Mother had gone back into the house, Dad was still experimenting. He placed a grasshopper, then a worm, then a hunk of cheese in front of the shell where the head had disappeared. As soon as we all drifted away, the head darted out. The long neck rose straight up so that the turtle could see in all directions and, of course, it spied Dad sneaking back.

Now nothing could tempt it out of its shell for the executioner's ax. I felt squeamish when Dad used pliers to reach into the shell and pull the head out for a mercifully quick blow. I sensed the difference between the death of this creature and that of the bothersome spiders and field mice. I knew it must have lived many years in our lake avoiding hazards, raising families, and somehow surviving the winters — perhaps tucked into the soft lake bottom near the point where we swam. I have forgotten the details of the dismembering of the turtle — perhaps I didn't watch — but I recall many yellow eggs in various sizes, still without firm shells, which added to the delicious flavor of the soup Dad produced with Mother's always supportive, if less enthusiastic, help.

"Would those eggs all have become baby turtles?" I asked.

"Yes," Dad said, "but many would have died or been eaten by big fish. Turtle mothers don't pay much attention once they've laid the eggs. Sometimes a dog digs them up."

"I didn't know turtles ever got so big," Bob remarked.

"Right. But even in a lake this big not many survive to her age. If they did, we wouldn't have many fish, I'm afraid. It all balances out." Even with spiders and field mice, nature had a plan. Guiltily, I enjoyed the soup along with the others. I comforted myself by arguing inwardly that it was no more cruel to make turtle soup than to eat the fish Dad caught almost every day. But the more I thought about it, the more I pictured that frightened turtle trying to hide in its snug shell home.

That experience was still in our minds as we grew older and began making pets of baby turtles. We raced our favorites on the front porch. One summer we invented a way to harness them to wagons made out of stiff typewriter paper. We passed many happy hours this way until the time Mother got up in the night and stepped on the cold, wet back of a tiny turtle that had escaped from its pan of water. I don't remember any hysterics, not even a scream. I do remember that keeping turtles in the house was thereafter quietly discouraged — although I heard Mother giggling as she told this story to a friend.

I had begged for a kitty, but cats were not popular on the island because they endangered the birds. We used our *Burgess Bird Book for Children* — as big as our family Bible — to build up a list of forty-three birds we had identified. We imitated the calls of the mourning dove and the cardinal well enough to get responses, and we learned to differentiate between the Baltimore and the orchard orioles, and among many of the finches. We watched and listened and learned. The saucy catbirds seemed to think they were mockingbirds. A kingfisher perched on the wire from our water windlass to the lake, then dropped like a rock into the water and flew back with crest bristling and a fish in his ungainly, swordlike beak. A redheaded woodpecker beat a tattoo on our metal stovepipe every morning at five until my dignified daddy, irritated beyond endurance, dashed out in his nightshirt, used his shotgun — and ruined the stovepipe. I was glad he hadn't killed the woodpecker. The hungry bird was only trying to find bugs to eat. But poor Dad needed his sleep, too, and now he had to replace the stovepipe. I wished I knew how to help. Maybe if I put some bugs out for the woodpecker? Who was right? Why was there never a real, for-sure answer?

Our parents wearied of the field mice that were so prolific when the grass on the Commons was not mowed. At the end of the summer, when we were returning to town, Mother removed from the kitchen every shred of food that might attract the mice, hoping they would confine themselves to the outdoors. Somehow she missed a package of rice, and the next year we found tiny hoards of it: in the toe of a tennis shoe, in a bureau drawer, in a mattress, in a dish in the cupboard, behind the clock, under the piano, on top of books in the bookcase. Each was accompanied by smelly black droppings.

The next year several islanders independently came to the conclusion that a cat left there over the winter would improve the situation. The cats did well and in their turn proliferated. An early visitor the following spring was horrified to find hungry, lean cats almost feral in their need. One sat on a fence post and leaped at anything in the surrounding territory that moved, whether bug or bird or mouse. We never entirely rid the island of field mice, but the population was greatly reduced by the cats and by mowing more of the grassy areas that were crisscrossed with their tunnels.

And where did those cats go when they were no longer needed? Into sacks with heavy stones, Bob whispered to me, and then to the lake bottom near the White Bridge. Bob also told me that once when he and Dad passed that place in the launch, the motor conked out. Dad mischievously suggested that the cats were taking their revenge. Having to end the cats' lives was a duty Dad obviously did not take lightly. A balance of sorts was restored, and we learned to live in watchful peace with mice and spiders *if* they stayed outdoors where they belonged.

I tried not to think about the cats.

A Haircut, Herons, and History

ONE FINE DAY at the beginning of the previous summer, when we were renters on the island, we were halfway to the north swimming beach when Mother noticed what Dad had done to her beloved firstborn's hair.

"Robert looks outrageous, Walter!" she exclaimed. "Please finish cutting his hair right after we swim." Once each summer, knowing how Bob enjoyed it, Mother agreed, albeit reluctantly, to my father's clipping off all the heavy black hair on my older brother's large, handsome head. This time Dad had allowed his imagination full play. As he clipped Bob's shiny scalp naked, he left bristly little clumps of hair to represent eyes, brows, nostrils, and lips. When Bob bent his head down so only the top showed, the effect was unnerving. Serious and soft-spoken, Bob nevertheless had a sense of mischief.

"I think it's great!" he gloated.

Mother and I were embarrassed by the haircut Dad gave Bob.

Everett approved everything his big brother said and agreed enthusiastically.

Although Mother wore an old knee-length, skirted brown wool bathing suit and her voice had an unaccustomed edge to it, she still projected daintiness and dignity. She was not averse to having a little fun, but she had not bargained for this grotesque face. Now others would be seeing him, not just family. I was glad I was a girl with Dutch bob secure. I shared her embarrassment.

Inconspicuous in a tan homemade cotton swimsuit about the same color as my plump, sun-tanned body, I had concealed my brown hair with its reddish glints under a white bathing cap. We often went with other islanders to the North End to enjoy the four o'clock arrival of the streetcar boat — the Yellow Canary, as everyone called it. It was one of six propeller-driven steam-powered boats, each accommodating 120 passengers, built in 1906 for the Twin City Rapid Transit Company. Streetcars capable of going sixty miles per hour left downtown Minneapolis via what was affectionately known as the "Line of Greenery and Scenery" and reached Excelsior, where they met the boats of the Yellow Fleet, designed and painted to resemble the streetcars. Wicker seats welcomed commuters and vacationers alike. Windows could be opened to catch the breezes as the handsome boats clipped along at twelve miles an hour. The awning-covered upper deck had benches fore and aft of the huge smokestack, which connected to the boiler of the coal-burning engine. In 1917 the boats provided our only convenient way to reach the island.

We watched the steamer come into sight belching smoke as it negotiated the buoys between Enchanted and Wawatasso Islands and pulled up at Crane Island's Big Dock. The purser sprang out and flung a thick hawser twice around the hefty dock post. Before he released the chain across the exit to allow passengers to alight, he dropped another rope in a clove hitch around a second twelve-inch-thick post at the other end of the L-shaped dock. The rope creaked and protested as the captain reversed the engine, stirring up spray and creating enticing whirlpools full of danger as the great craft shuddered to a standstill, snugged neatly against the dock.

Mother shepherded us children into the shallow water near shore while Dad joined some of the other islanders on the wide dock, which extended twenty feet or so from the land to the drop-off. There, water eighteen feet deep accommodated the steamer. Swimmers liked to dive from the four-foot-high dock and used a ladder on the side to climb back to safety, thus avoiding the muddy, treacherous lake bottom. As the steamboat pulled away from the dock, the bravest among them dared to dive into the churning water roiled by the boat's powerful propeller. A couple of them were once permitted to dive from the upper deck of the boat itself. They enjoyed being pummeled and tossed to and fro and even turned upside down by the force of the twisting currents.

I noticed Dad standing alone. Even in his striped, skirted bathing suit he had a special grace. He was my romantic idea of a foreigner — after all, his name was Walter Raleigh, and some of his friends called him Sir Walter. He was courtly, a little formal, but friendly and courteous. His hair was brown, his shaggy eyebrows yellow, and his well-trimmed mustache red. Once, Mother told us, he grew a beard, but it too was bright red. They laughed together and agreed it must be cut off at once. When we begged him to grow one again so we could see it, he said his hair had been sandy when he was a kid, and we should have seen him then. He joked, but he never again let his whiskers grow.

As the purser released the boat that day to continue southeast past Eagle Island across the bay, I saw Dad turn and notice a passenger who was staring with an agonized expression at our little family in the shallows. Bob had ducked under the water, held his breath, and exposed just the top of his head to the gaze of the shocked passengers. What kind of monster was this? they must have wondered. Dad was at first startled, slightly abashed, then amused; he dared not look at Mother.

Meanwhile, I had wandered to the end of the dock, where I could watch the diving. I loved the north end of the island. The twenty-foot bluffs fell abruptly away to a low, smooth, grassy lawn surrounded on three sides by tall, dark elms. To me, it was a fairy circle, and I populated it with elfin creatures from my storybooks. Dreaming, I leaned against the smooth dock post just out of the way of the swimmers, now running the dock's full length to throw themselves headlong into the deep water.

Zenas Clark Dickinson, a young professor who, like us, was a relative newcomer to the island community, sprinted to the end of the dock. As he reached full speed, he spotted a swimmer in the water just below. Frantic to avoid landing on the swimmer, he reached out to stop himself by grabbing the dock post — and got me instead. We both tumbled into the water. Aghast, Mother left Everett with Bob and ran to dive in where I had disappeared. When they didn't see me come up, she and Dad and four or five others who were already in the water began swimming around wildly and porpoise-diving to hunt for my body. Perhaps they pictured me already stuck in the soft muddy silt of the lake floor. Zeke, himself a father, kept swimming in ever larger circles, peering down with his face under water, his long skinny arms and legs splashing in a frenzy.

He had released me as soon as he realized what he had done, hoping against hope that I would not fall. Without his continuing momentum, I tumbled into the deep water close to the dock. Abruptly wrenched from my musing, disoriented by the sudden sense of falling, then the noisy splash and the cool ducking, I nevertheless surged promptly to the surface. I found myself under the dock, out of easy sight of my would-be rescuers. Dad had taught me to put my face under and breathe out to make bubbles the year before, and then I'd learned to dog-paddle. Now considering myself a veteran swimmer at age five, I had no time to be frightened and began to enjoy the forbidden adventure. The bracing under the dock formed a small enclosure, a little "house," and the water-filtered light gave it a strange glow. I explored a bit before swimming out to the ladder, where Mother immediately spied me. She smiled as she hurried to me with a self-satisfied look, as if all the time she had expected me to breathe out and make bubbles. Dad got to me first and greeted me with a quiet, re-assuring "Nicely done, Miggles!"

When Dad had first called me Miggles, he remarked that it rhymed with giggles. The nickname never caught on with anyone else, and somehow I got the message that he wished I were a more vivacious, spontaneous child — less inclined to watch and wonder. Now he was pleased with me. He calmed the others, suggesting that after this we all take turns in diving for safety's sake. He thereby short-circuited the attention that had, to my surprise and delight, focused on me. Before this I had felt I had importance only as "one of the Myers kids who swim like fish without any fear." Now I had new fame as "the child not yet in kindergarten who fell into deep water and it didn't faze her." And the next day I was the proud recipient of a box of candy from the penitent Mr. Dickinson.

Our walk back to the cottage took us the length of the Commons. It was beautiful in the late-afternoon sunshine. Before 1906, perhaps even before the Dakota Indians named this area Mini-tonka ("big water"), the island had been densely populated by great blue herons, commonly called cranes, and by smaller, fast-flying hooded cormorants. Forks in the tall hardwoods bore the birds' ragged, loosely constructed nests sixty feet high, and early in May the parents took turns covering three or four bluish-green eggs. Later they shared the chores of fishing and regurgitating food for the fledglings. Birds often sat rigid like sentinels at the ends of the branches, frightening away anyone who might have stopped at the island. But after a tornado felled the island trees, the heronry moved to Wawatasso, an unoccupied nearby island owned by the state. There were other small unoccupied islands, such as Goose Island and Pelican Island, but most islands of any size — including Enchanted, Shady, Big, Phelps, and Eagle — had dwellings.

The uninhabited island where the birds now nested was infinitely mysterious and inviting to us children. It had high bluffs and a swampy place in the middle. There was a harbor with arms reaching out toward Eagle Island. When we paddled our canoe between these two islands, we could see sacks of concrete and sand arranged in rows under the water leading from the point of Eagle north toward Wawa. We had been told that the owner of Eagle hoped the waves would build up a connecting sandbar so that he could claim Wawa as part of his island. We were inclined to believe this because we had observed the pilings he used around the other point of his island, which stretched south toward Gallagher's Point on the mainland. This point he filled in with dirt and concrete to increase the length of that part of his land. As I sat in the canoe and passed these points, questions spun themselves through my sun-filled mind. How could people be so selfish? And when they already had so much? Could they get away with it? Weren't there laws? Didn't they know God would know?

We had several times visited Wawatasso to explore the interior. I stayed quiet and close to my father on these treks, for I had heard rumors that there was a "blind pig" there. A wild, uncontrolled animal might charge down the bank toward the noise we made. I imagined sightless red eyes behind every tree. Years later, I discovered that blind pig was a term for a speakeasy. At one time, fishermen told Dad, there were sheep on Wawa, with no shepherd. We found no evidence of them — only wood ticks, flat brown ticks that, if they aren't picked off promptly, swell up with stolen blood. They have to be twisted off counterclockwise or treated with kerosene or fingernail polish to asphyxiate them. Mother examined us minutely when we returned.

Once late that summer we came home from Wawatasso with something more than wood ticks. Wild grapes grew in profusion there, the vines draped over bushes and low tree branches. Mother boiled the purple grapes, pressed them through a colander, and produced a marvelously tart, tasty jelly we vastly preferred to the relatively mild confection from the store. A diligent cleanup followed, for utensils, sink, dishcloths, and hands had absorbed a stubborn, deep purple stain.

Wawatasso was later used as a Boy Scout campground for many years, but its greatest appeal for all of us was the big birds — the noisy cormorants and especially the cranes. We often saw the three-foot and four-foot bluish-gray birds stalking fish and frogs in the shallows near the reeds. I watched in envy whenever I saw one rise with slow, effortless wing beat and amazing wingspread. The bird would draw up its reedlike legs, point them straight back like a rudder, and look down searchingly from the buoyant cushions of air, neck folded in.

We moved back to town before the birds gathered for their fall migration, but I often tried to imagine it. A friend who lived on the mainland once told my parents about hearing a great commotion at Wawa as he rowed home from an evening of fishing in the reeds. Quietly putting up his oars, he let himself drift close to shore. For hours he listened in amazement as the majestic birds gathered in restless groups. Their preflight bedlam continued all night, and our friend stayed and stayed, unable to believe what he was seeing and hearing.

He said it was like a continuous committee meeting, erupting into quarrels that subsided as decisions apparently were made. The birds flew to new perches as if to press new causes. At night their gray feathers showed only as dark shapes in the gloom, but the excitement was evident in their restlessness. He also told us that in May the birds returned in flocks that darkened the sky. The sound of their wings was eerie, and their presence ominous.

They cluttered the air with their raucous cries as they swooped untidily onto the lake, he said. Hungry, they went fishing at once, driving the small fish, surrounding them, plucking them from the water, and feeding. The birds were noisy until contests for male dominance finally were resolved and they settled down to hunting frogs and fish, snakes, and water beetles as they raised their young.

We could believe stories we had heard that Dakota people drew maps for early white explorers that left the Minnetonka area blank: they wanted to keep it for themselves. After the Civil War, Lake Minnetonka was a popular recreational area among people from the East and South and later for upper- and middle-class Minneapolitans in this era before the automobile. Until the storm-induced move of the big birds, Crane Island escaped development.

Gradually we learned the history of Crane Island. Mr. Charles E. Woodward had been spending a summer vacation at the nearby town of Mound. Curious about the island after the storm of 1906, he explored there and found it surprisingly free from contamination by the big birds and ideally suited for cottages. His friend Merton S. Amy accompanied him as he explored and surveyed the island. Woodward and a few friends from the Bethlehem Presbyterian Church of Minneapolis in 1907 formed the nonprofit Crane Island Association, purchased the island, divided it into lots, and began to build. They later offered space to outsiders, subject to the approval of the association. Purchasers could use the Great Northern rail connection to Mound or Spring Park and hire a private boat to make the twenty-five-minute trip to the island, or they could use the Yellow Canaries, which at that time made two regular daily stops at Crane Island.

The streetcar system and boats opened up the lake to middle-class city dwellers and to the Minnesota custom of a summer place at the lake. The area changed little during and after World War I, when we summered there.

I'm not sure how Dad found out about Crane Island, but he told me that his father remonstrated with him at his extravagance in borrowing to invest in the property — and this only two years after joining the University of Minnesota faculty. It was hard for me to think of Dad as having been chided by a parent, his judgment questioned.

Dad had taught German at Miami University in Oxford, Ohio, where the boys and I were born. When we moved to Minneapolis, we rented for a year at 1629 University Avenue. Dad and seven-year-old Bob spent Saturdays walking a mile to the eight-room house we had purchased at 608 Oak Street Southeast. They made repairs, replaced gas fixtures with electrical ones, and shellacked the fine stairway in the front hall. Dad taught us to walk upstairs on our toes "like Indians" to protect his handiwork, the first of many expert jobs he based on what he had learned from his carpenter father. These projects provided a welcome change from his university work, and he eagerly tackled the new summer challenges of putting in the dock, keeping

Our house in Minneapolis, near the university

up the boats, and installing a drain for water from the sink, as well as studying out the best fishing spots and lures.

At the lake, when Dad was working on a new project, he often sat with brow wrinkled in concentration over his intense, deep-set blue eyes and pulled in a twisting motion on his luxuriant eyebrows. We did not disturb him then, nor if anything went wrong when he was working. If the work went well, we were sometimes allowed to help, although this privilege usually went to Bob. When Dad taught a new dive or a game or held us spellbound with a made-up story, he was completely ours.

Dad taught us table blessings in German and carefully monitored our accents. When he tucked us into bed, he sometimes told us the stories of great German operas. Once when he told the story of a complicated Wagnerian opera, Ev asked what an opera was. Dad had been working on the roof earlier, and the ladder still leaned against the house. He climbed a few steps and demonstrated.

"I am the hero," he explained, "and I need a hammer. The house is about to come down around my ears if I can't fix this one beam. So, instead of asking for a hammer, I throw a black cape around my shoulders, swell out my chest, and sing."

And he did. In full voice, beginning low and working up the scale in thirds, he bellowed, "Give me, give me, give me," and then in a burst in the tenor range, "a ham, a ham, only a ham, just one ham, please give me a ham, a ham, a hammer!" Somehow he finished at a thrilling, rumbling low bass while we collapsed in laughter.

Mother sometimes mildly urged him to sit down and take pleasure in what he had worked so hard to create.

Putting in the dock always was Dad's first chore of the season.

She was able to manage her own chores, even when she entertained guests, without losing the serenity that always seemed to surround her. When she sat in the sunshine on the front porch to read, she often tucked her tiny feet under her, her small head bent over her book. She occasionally looked up to watch a bird fluttering in the kinnikinnick bushes or to let her eyes rest as she enjoyed the view from under the great elms. Her gentle hands with their long, flat fingers were ready if a child appeared at her knee with a scratch or hurt feelings.

We had no car in those years, of course. We depended on the streetcars, one of which turned south off Oak Street just half a block east of our home near the university. Oak Street extended seven or eight blocks, from East River Road to the university stadium. There the streetcar swerved north to the campus and downtown. This remarkable transportation network stretched forty miles northeast from Minneapolis to White Bear and Stillwater and twenty-five miles west to Lake Minnetonka. The fare to the lake was twenty-five cents. By 1917 the fleet of six steamboats provided hourly service—for only ten cents—from mid-May through September to twenty-seven landings around both the upper and lower lakes. Crane Island was the most westerly and farthest from Excelsior, which was on the Lower Lake where the boats met the streetcars. We took the boat service for granted, assuming it would be there whenever we needed it.

We knew nothing then of the luxurious hotels that before the turn of the century accommodated wealthy southerners who came in vast numbers to escape the heat and

The Hopkins *was part of the Yellow Fleet that was our reliable connection to the mainland.*

fevers. They enjoyed excellent cuisine and fabulous settings as well as the beauties of Lake Minnetonka. "Every room on a verandah" was the slogan for the elegant Tonka Bay Hotel. James J. Hill's Lafayette Hotel was described as a palace with one hundred rooms. Hotel St. Louis at Deephaven housed an exclusive summer clientele of four hundred aristocrats from the Deep South. Their "colored" servants stayed in a row of cabins behind the hotel. Twin Cities people also enjoyed extravagant dinners and dances there, and a streetcar waited till the "hop" was over to take them home. These hotels and many others flourished until the financial crash of 1893. After that more people from the rapidly expanding middle class were attracted to the lake and began to invest in property there.

Only the Sampson House of Excelsior survived. The Big Island Park was an amusement park that attracted summer visitors in the years from 1906 to 1911, but this, too, was before our time. The agony of the World War had seemed remote on the island, although Dad, as a teacher of German and with a German name, at first felt somewhat suspect there. The memory of the sinking of the *Lusitania* and Germany's prowling of the seas, forcing our entry into the war, was still strong. Hostilities were formally concluded in November 1918, and wartime feelings began to fade.

From our front porch we occasionally glimpsed sailboats from the Wayzata Yacht Club as they bent to the breezes rounding nearby Eagle Island at the far end of their racecourse. But for the most part, Crane Island was isolated: no bridge to the mainland, no store, no telephone, no electricity, and grocery delivery just twice a week. Only the Yellow Canary made a link, more fragile than we realized, to civilization. The island was a retreat rather than a resort, and we depended on the lake and on each other for our enjoyment — and sometimes for a haircut.

Three Times of Danger

"YES, YES! I CAN COME." How lucky I felt as the school year drew to a close before our third summer on Crane Island. I had been afraid I would miss Gayle Priester's eighth birthday party, but he had finally set it for the Friday afternoon before our Saturday move to the lake. Gayle was also fond of my dearest pal and constant companion, Ruth Burkhard, and we attended the party together, she in a red sweater and matching skirt and I wearing a pleated blue skirt and a blue blouse with a white collar.

The week after the festivities I did not feel so lucky. As usual, my brothers and I met the three o'clock streetcar boat, but to our great surprise, our father, who was finishing his spring quarter of teaching, was not there. Something must have delayed him. We met him at the five o'clock boat, and he hugged us hard with his city jacket carefully folded over one arm, but he seemed preoccupied and not as full of fun as we expected. When we reached home, I noticed that he and Mother began to talk earnestly. She looked at me strangely. Her look was loving, but anxious too. Hearing the name Priester, I felt bold enough to ask what they were talking about.

Dad hesitated a moment, then explained, "Marjorie, one of the boys who was at Gayle's party has come down with smallpox. As you know, that is very contagious, so I am going to vaccinate all you children right now — to keep you well."

Little children were not routinely vaccinated in those days, but we all had heard how helpless people became in an epidemic and how quickly they could develop the angry pustules that might kill them or at least disfigure their faces and bodies with pocks. Rather than arrange to get us to a Minneapolis doctor, Dad had gone to the Red Cross, learned how to vaccinate, and purchased supplies. Since the virus could have spread from me to my brothers, he vaccinated all three of us that afternoon, carefully swabbing our arms and using packaged needles and measured doses.

We didn't really have time to think about the vaccination, nor to dread the prick of the sharp needles, and Dad was skillful. The job was quickly done, and the boys went back to assembling their metal Meccano pieces in an elaborate creation. My stomach rebelled at supper, and before Mother could get me to bed, I was vomiting. She rubbed my back, which had begun to ache, and found that I had a degree and a half of temperature.

That made things look altogether different. "Am I going to die, Mommy, because I went to the party? Am I going to get awful holes in my face? I don't want to go to heaven alone. Will my brothers go with me?"

"I think your tummy is a little upset from the excitement, dear. You'll feel much better in the morning." Mother refused to acknowledge dangers that were not yet proven.

My parents must have struggled with dark thoughts and fears that night, but Mother's assurance proved to be correct. By morning I felt completely recovered, and by noon I was hungry and ready for play. The boys had no symptoms until two or three days later, when they, too, were nauseated. As it turned out, they were reacting to the vaccination — but I developed several red pox on the palms of my hands and the soles of my feet. I had smallpox!

The health officer from Mound came to the island in his city suit and nailed a red cardboard sign to the house. We were under quarantine. Apparently the vaccination — in spite of being tardy — had helped. I continued to feel good, and no more lesions developed. But my imprisonment restricted the whole family; I felt guilty and unclean. When Dad took us for a canoe ride to break the monotony of our confinement, I worried for fear the breeze might carry my infection to people on the shore.

Dad was with us all day early that summer. Since he was assigned to teach only one session of summer school, he had plenty of time to rehabilitate a big inboard launch that had weathered in the weeds for some years. He had purchased it for almost nothing from Mr. Hermann, one of the original islanders. Following instructions in a book from the library, Dad scraped off the crumbling white paint, then dug the cracks between the boards out clean and la-

The launch, steady and slow

boriously caulked them, forcing a fluffy, stringlike stuff into the cracks with a chisel and knife.

When the reconditioned boat was launched, it had been caulked so firmly that it could not soak up the water it needed to expand the wood to make it perfectly watertight. We always carried a hand bilge pump to rid the boat of the water that collected underneath the floorboards around the engine. We took turns "pumping out."

The massive engine was made by the White company. I knew nothing about mechanics, but I heard the boys call it a "make and break" engine. I wondered if it had come close to breaking Dad. Though he finally got it to work, it continued to be unpredictable about starting. Dad usually had us quickly on our way. He opened a small petcock on the side of the cylinder, squirted gasoline into the tiny cup, closed the latch, fitted the heavy iron handle onto the flywheel, and cranked. If the engine balked, he began to chew his lips. His scowl deepened. I can see him bending over that big black "one-lunger" — one cylinder — machine, sweat dripping from his nose and chin in spite of the red bandanna tied around his head. We children became silent — seeking to be not seen and not heard — as he cranked. Eventually the engine coughed, stopped, then caught and stalled, and at last settled into a steady, noisy beat, and the tension broke. His shirt soaked, Dad settled down happily at the rear steering wheel, his mind again on some new cove to explore or discovery to watch for as we went about our errands.

On the other hand, there were times I saw him crank and crank and choke the engine using the little petcock, until patience and strength were exhausted. An awed silence descended over us when once in exasperation he threw down that heavy crank against the unbudging flywheel. I saw frustration in his face, disappointment after the long hours of working on the motor. Something made me want to touch him, to tell him it didn't matter, we could go another time — but I sat silent, tense, unsure of what to do. Even Dad had his limits, it seemed.

Apparently we kids had limits to our patience, too. The long quarantine was telling on all of us. Often I sat in the high swing Dad had hung for us between two tall trees. It was at the foot of the sloping lot; beyond it the ground fell sharply away. When Dad reached to his full height and even jumped a little to push me high above his head, the effect made me giddy — I seemed to be soaring away from the earth, which was also falling away beneath me.

Once I ran to my daddy when he was swinging Helen Jane McKendry. Was I jealous? What could have possessed

The land fell away from our big swing, making the swinger feel she was going out over the lake.

me to run into the swing after all his warnings? He managed to deflect the swing and slow it down, but it socked me on the side of my face, bloodying my nose. The burst of pain was a shock, and the blow seemed to echo in my head. Dad carried me to the house and made me lie down, still weeping softly, while Mother put cold compresses on my nose. I enjoyed their attention, but I was not able to forget that the accident was my fault. An unsightly bruise reminded me of that fact, and I chided myself, thinking Bob never would have done anything so stupid.

Another day I swung lazily in my bathing suit as I waited for Dad to finish transplanting a barberry bush. Everett was playing nearby wearing only his shorts, also ready to swim. Perhaps he felt I had overstayed my turn in the swing. He found some soft yellowish punk from the inside of a fallen tree. As I reached the low point of the glide, he threw a small piece of punk over my head. His timing was good. A moment earlier or later and it would have struck me.

"Watch out!" I warned. "You almost hit me!"

"Ha, Scaredy, I never!" he replied.

Cocky and sure of his skill, he continued to torment me, and I complained loudly. It made no difference. Again and again his arm went back and another piece of punk came flying toward me. Finally the inevitable happened, and one hit me in the forehead. Unhurt but outraged, I slipped out of the swing and went wailing to my father. To my surprise, he seemed to be irritated with both of us. He cut a slender willow switch and lightly whacked our legs with it three times.

"But Daddy—"

"Now be quiet, both of you!"

Horrified and now crying in earnest, I ran inside. My mother must have been watching from the kitchen window.

"Why? Why?" I wailed. "I was being good. I wasn't hurting anyone."

She bent down. I showed her the red welts coming on my legs and cried anew. Her sweet face showed distress. She couldn't bear to see a hurt. Now she'd commiserate with me about Daddy, I thought.

But she didn't. Neither did she scold me. I snuggled up to her, but she only pointed to Daddy, working again in the heat. "He doesn't like to hear whining," she said. "He works so hard for us. He likes us to be happy."

Now I realize the conflict of loyalties Mother must have been feeling. Parents should not criticize each other in front of the children. Parents must present a solid front. How tempted she must have been to put her arms around me, for she surely sensed my bewilderment and feeling of abandonment.

The sting of the willow switch quickly faded, but the sting of what seemed like rejection lingered as I wandered outside. I had been selfish about the swing and noisy in my whining, but still Ev had no right to throw things at me. It seemed it was best to just keep a low profile when Dad was under pressure. Soon Dad finished with the bushes, and we all traipsed to the water together. I don't recall that our feelings about this incident were ever talked out. I tucked my hurt away to think about later.

Another day when the quarantine hung heavy on us all, Dad with a gleam in his eye got out his map of the lake, Mother packed a lunch, and we set out for a luxurious all-day trip to enjoy the new-old launch. We chugged away from the island, through the narrow channels and between islands, past lovely homes on the mainland. I went to my favorite place on the front deck, slid my legs under a shiny low railing, and splashed my feet in the collar of spray plowed up by the prow. I dreamed along contentedly and singing a little song: "Every little wave has its night cap on / Night cap, white cap, night cap on." The boys hated it. From the back deck Bob and Everett dragged toy boats, which they had laboriously chiseled from blocks of wood (and which became increasingly elaborate each year), watching critically how they rode the small waves of our wake. They, too, had a railing for safety.

We circled the Upper Lake, and Dad pointed out landmarks from his map until finally we reached the Narrows, which leads to the Lower Lake. There we looped back and approached tiny, unoccupied Goose Island. Dad cut the motor and let Bob throw out the anchor. In the distance a catboat dipped and stalled in the fitful breeze. We ate deviled eggs, peanut butter sandwiches on homemade bread, and tomatoes, which we gobbled with juice dripping over our chins as we hung over the side of the boat. We finished with oatmeal cookies with lots of fat raisins. The sun was hot, and we relished the iced lemonade, carefully apportioned, for its tart coolness. We had never before ventured so far on the beautiful lake.

As we cruised toward home, we came upon a vast array of white water lilies. Beyond them, nearer the shore, the smaller yellow lilies rose stiffly above the waves. I begged to pick just a few. Dad was dubious: the tough, thick stems of the lily pads could tangle on the propeller blades. He hesitated. Mother put in a word for me, and the launch eased toward the nearest white flower. I leaned and caught it, but its stem was like spongy rubber, and Dad's strong pull was needed to loosen it from its muddy moorings.

He passed it to me, then another, and I held them in my hands reverently. Each of the dripping flowers was as big as a saucer. Now we had drifted into the midst of the lilies, and I was in raptures. The petals shone so white, in such perfect array around the pistils and stamens. A marvelous God seemed very close. I wondered how many blades of grass He had planted on all those islands—and on the mainland, and in all the whole world. A lovely sense of peace stole over me.

Soon the afternoon sunshine began to feel uncomfortably hot, and I became aware that not everyone was as happy as I with this side trip into the lilies. The launch's reverse gear was not dependable, and we had gradually drifted deeper into the dense growth of flowers. Their snakelike stems had tangled on the propeller. The engine sputtered and stopped. Dad sighed resignedly, but, since we were already in trouble, he let us pick a few more of the beautiful blossoms. Then he went to the back deck and glumly stashed his glasses, shed his shirt, lay on his stomach, and reached under the boat to break the strangling stems off the propeller. One clump refused to come loose even with Dad's increasingly exasperated jerks and pulls. Sweating, with his bare shoulders burning in the hot sun, he prepared to start the engine again. Mother suggested that we use the boat hook to paddle and pole our way to clear water first. Then, with Dad biting his lips and holding Bob's legs, my brother plunged his head and upper body underwater to free the prop from the last tightly wound clump of stems. I was proud of Bob, but I felt guilty when I saw him coughing. My request got us into this trouble. I clutched the precious flowers and, leaning over the side of the boat, scooped up water to sprinkle them and keep them cool and fresh till we got home.

As I often did when problems seemed too big, I began to ponder an escape fantasy. What would I find if I slipped into the water here? The side of a silvery fish flashed briefly and disappeared again into the twining stems. Langorous and sleepy, I felt an irresponsible urge to follow, to trade my drab shorts for shiny scales and gills and sink into the cool green waters. Would I find elusive friends among the lilies as the children did in my book *The Water-Babies?* Would there be no feeling guilty and not quite knowing why? I didn't really know what I had done wrong. I loved flowers the way Dad loved to fish, Mom loved to read, and the boys enjoyed fooling with motors. It was confusing.

If I were a water baby and lived among the lilies, there would be no little brother teasing and no big brother always outshining me. There would be no Daddy looking irritated and Mother unhappy. Everything would be easy and pleasant, and the cool, cool water would always be comforting.

Sometime during that long quarantine I had an experience so frightening that I was sure it would never leave my memory.

I was standing alone on the front porch, awed and unbelieving as I looked out at the lake and the darkening skies. A scary stifling quiet had given way to a buffeting wind from the west that struck the cottage from behind with threatening force and noisy gusts of cold rain. My eyes never left the lake. I shivered a little in my light clothing. Squalls darkened the water in patches, racing crazily across the lake, moving like the mercury we once spilled from a broken thermometer.

Beyond the shelter of the shore, the wind drove waves into peaks, then savagely whipped off their tops. Spray mingled with the rain and scudded viciously over the surface. The cottage shook. I pictured its being picked up, swept through the bushes, and splashed into the angry waters. Then I felt Dad's hand on my shoulder. I pressed against him and, trembling, told him my anxieties. He listened and soberly considered the possibilities. He gave me no false promises, just told me he had tended to the windows, secured the boats, and done what he could to be ready for an emergency. His reassuring presence made me feel that we could manage whatever came, or at least be ready to do our best as we were so often admonished to do.

When the storm had blown itself out, we all five walked barefoot through the soggy grass to the west side of the island. Leaf bits and broken twigs and branches were scattered everywhere. Then we saw what had happened. A giant maple tree, one we had climbed many times, had split and crashed down. Some of the broken branches had pierced the ground, and they held the splintery halves of the redolent yellow bole suspended horizontally. Ev began at once to explore, but Bob, like me, stood quiet and said nothing. I felt sad, and my big brother had a faraway look on his face, as he did sometimes when he strummed on his banjo. Maybe he, too, thought of this tree as a friend.

Once more during that lonely quarantine, I had a scary experience with the forces of nature. I was lying on the front porch bed while an electrical storm lit the sky again and again. I counted the seconds between lightning and thunder and realized the strikes were close. Then suddenly I felt as if my wrists and throat were going to burst and even felt a little faint. Shocked and amazed, I ran to the kitchen to tell Mother. When she and I explored later, we found a burned place in the grass in the Eustises' front yard where lightning had blackened an area a few feet across at the foot of a tree it had struck. It was barely twenty feet from where I had been lying.

I was glad when the quarantine that had seemed so long was finally lifted. Three times I had escaped danger, and I understood anew that I was a lucky girl. I was sobered.

Was it because I was lonely during those long days that I remember it all so vividly?

Blackie

BOB AND EVERETT and I had long wanted a dog and teased as much as we dared to achieve that end. My constant begging had gotten me a kitten named Snowball. A town friend of Mother's let me choose one from a half-grown litter and agreed to take it back in the fall, when, she assured me, I could come visit to ease the separation. Everyone played with my Snowball — even Mother, who had never had a kitten in her childhood home — but my brothers were still dissatisfied.

Sympathizing with our desire for pets and perhaps also wishing for an inexpensive change from a largely fish diet, Dad experimented one summer with Belgian hares. He explained that they are really a large domestic rabbit. He bought two females and a male and proposed to raise young for meat. A summer seems a short time for such an enterprise, even on a small, experimental scale, but the boys and I willingly undertook their care and feeding. When they were in their pen, we studied their constantly moving noses and mouths and whiskers, framed by their long floppy ears. If we let them out of the enclosure, they dispersed in three directions. Surprisingly vigorous, they covered ground rapidly with their erratic, leaping gait. Their dark gray fur was soft and long, and their skin seemed loose on their bodies.

And we fed them. We learned to rejoice that their pen had been placed conveniently close to the garden, for they ate constantly. We were soon uncomfortably busy foraging for them. When we wanted to go off and play, we had to store up food in their pen. We picked dandelion greens and long grass. We harvested radish tops and cabbage leaves. We pulled weeds, and when our own supply ran out, we offered our services to the neighbors. One day Bob, desperate, remembered the gravel pit, where furry-leaved mullein grew tall and rank. Together we pulled armfuls of the plant. The rabbits attacked it as enthusiastically as they accepted all the food we offered, but, alas, it was poisonous for them. My parents said they acted as if they were intoxicated. They hopped a little way, then tumbled over, soon picked themselves up and tried again. We didn't know how to help them, and when one of them died, we were left with a miserable feeling of guilt. I tried to hide from myself a feeling of relief that the foraging chores would be reduced.

Perhaps it was the male that died. In any case, the other two slowly recovered but never produced any young. By the end of the summer, we children were much too attached to them to regard them other than as pets. Supposedly Dad came to regret his mercenary ambitions because nothing was ever again mentioned about butchering them. In the fall they mysteriously disappeared without explanation. Bob suspected that Dad shot and buried them — there seemed to be no other way out when we moved to town.

We felt as if we didn't really deserve another pet but continued to tease for a dog. Apparently our eventual triumph was the result of behind-the-scenes bargaining between my parents. Dad, as usual, was all for new adventures and learning experiences. Mother preferred keeping things simple, with a chance for an occasional quiet afternoon on the porch with a book. She was certainly right about one thing: a dog could be a nuisance.

We children could think of nothing else the day Dad had arranged with a Minneapolis friend to bring a dog to Zumbra Heights, where we had left the boat for him. He told us later that Blackie was completely unnerved by his initiation to island life. He flattened himself on the floor of the launch, as far as possible from the engine, and remained so for the crossing. He would not be comforted until Dad gently lifted him out and into Bob's waiting arms.

Blackie followed us children everywhere — except into the house. And it was understood from the beginning that he was ours only for the summer. When fall came, he must be returned to the dog pound whence he came. Our parents warned us how difficult the parting would be, but in our joy we readily agreed to the condition.

Blackie was a slender, shorthaired, average-sized dog. He was pretty, loving, reasonably obedient, but I fear not overly bright. Of course, he had no training and frolicked as freely as we did.

Blackie was the dog I had always wanted.

Crane Island became his home, but the cottage was forbidden territory. We knew, and soon he did, too, that he was to sleep outdoors; he found shelter underneath the porch when it rained. One of my vivid memories of Blackie is watching him breathlessly sprinting around the cottage, as if on a racetrack. One day he had been following the boys when they vanished into the cottage through the kitchen door, picked up a toy boat, and unexpectedly left via the front porch. They ran down to the dock, where they were out of Blackie's sight, and to his chagrin our pet was left waiting by the kitchen door. Ever after, he attacked the un-solvable problem of monitoring the front and back doors simultaneously by doing his best to arrive at both at the same time, and he very nearly succeeded. Banks of earth gradually built up at each corner as he slanted his body like a bobsled in full careening flight. Dad's efforts to repair the lawn at those points were temporary and in the end fruitless.

There were times, as I guess there are with all dogs, when atavistic impulses came over Blackie. Inexplicably, he would disappear, then return in high spirits but with an odor that was truly unspeakable. More than once we caught him rolling on a dead fish. He rolled again and again, rubbing his whole body in the disgusting, disintegrating remains, clearly enjoying it, until he was unthinkable as a companion. Whether he was really more loving after his indiscretions I wasn't sure, but it seemed so. It took all three of us and a session at the lake with soap and a scrubbing brush to make him bearable again. Mother sent one of us to bury the remains of the fish deep in the sand. She claimed she could discern traces of Blackie's indulgences for days.

Otherwise, if my brothers and I were outside the house, Blackie was with us. When we climbed trees, Blackie lay below. When we had treats, Blackie shared them. He gloried in sticky peanut butter, which he attempted to scrub off the roof of his mouth with his long tongue; we laughed to see him try to get at it by rubbing his paw along his nose. He dodged the swing when we pumped up, and he chased our tennis balls. When we visited the outhouse, Blackie guarded the door. When we swam, Blackie paddled along with us, snorting water out of his nose, climbing with our help onto the barge, and allowing himself to be dumped off in our games.

I had visions of having to protect Snowball, but I needn't have worried. Blackie loved everyone, including the cat. It was Snowball who spit and clawed at Blackie's first overtures, but she was soon allowing him to lie down next to her. Finally he could take her head in his mouth and gently drag her from place to place while she continued to purr contentedly.

Dad was less a part of our activities that summer. Because of the war, fewer students were studying German, and Dad, as one of the newer professors on the German faculty, agreed to change to the field of economics. Many days he went out on the lake alone in one of the boats. He carried among his books an economics text and many papers, and he stayed away hours at a time.

For us young ones, life went on pretty much as usual. In the times Dad spent with us, he was as lively and interested as ever. Mother did her best to conceal the strain he was under and to fill the vacuum when he was preparing for classes called Money and Banking, Business Cycle, and Basic Theory of Economics.

My mind followed my dad out onto the lake. Sometimes I looked longingly after him and at the trees and clouds peacefully reflected in the lake — placid until his crisp pulls on the oars made little whirlpools that crinkled the surface, distorting the images.

It happened that when Dad was at the university and the boys were away somewhere with friends, the lake tempted Mother and me to paddle to Enchanted Island by ourselves to visit our friends the Perines, who had daughters near my age. We even donned cotton dresses for our jaunt, making it a real celebration. But we had not taken Blackie into consideration. He had forgotten his earlier terror of boats and expected to go along. With none of the family at the cottage, he apparently assumed it was his right — nay, his duty — to accompany us. When we thought we had finally chased him away, we quickly wrestled the canoe to the water and pushed off. He jumped out of the bushes, up onto the dock, and into the canoe. I stepped back into the shallow water and lifted him out, shoved the canoe off, and hopped in again.

We were free at last — or so we thought. He followed us the length of the island along the shore, scrambling over docks and around fences and boats on the beaches. When we reached the North End, our course took us out into open water. This was the farthest point to which he could follow, and he disappeared, presumably to go back home. We had no sooner congratulated ourselves than he suddenly emerged from the tall reeds that grew twenty feet out toward Enchanted Island, bravely striking out into the bay, where the waves made him hold his head high. We couldn't leave him. How could we turn him around? We waited, and he came up beside the canoe. I was paddling stern, and I reached with my long paddle to try to point him once more toward home. I clumsily caught a wave that splashed into his face. Blackie choked. I panicked. I was sure he would drown. What could I do? I knelt and helped him scrabble into the boat.

Mother and I were as far apart as it is possible to get in a canoe, but when Blackie shook himself, he showered us both. He was thorough. He shook again and again until our laboriously ironed dresses hung limp. Blackie showed his appreciation by barking and bounding excitedly from one of us to the other. By the time he was calm enough to lie down, the festive feeling of our little adventure was gone. But Blackie was safe, which suddenly seemed very important.

Having established his right to be one of us when we went canoeing, Blackie joined us one evening when Dad, eager to enjoy the outdoors after a hot trip to the city, suggested that we have our supper on the lake. As usual, we spread the cork-filled cushions from the long launch benches on the bottom of the spacious canoe. They fit nicely between the two hinged lazybacks that rested against the thwarts in the belly of the boat. Mother, in her long skirt and ruffled blouse, and I sat side by side, traveling backward, and the boys, legs intertwined with ours, faced us. Dad occupied the small stern seat from which he lazily guided us across the lake toward Eagle Island. The evening was calm, so he did not need a paddler in front. Blackie stood still as a figurehead in the prow, looking down at the quiet water.

Mother, waiting just a bit impatiently for Dad to find a place to drift and eat, distributed our supper. She passed out paper plates, then sandwiches and peaches. Carrot sticks and radishes from the garden followed. She cautiously filled paper cups with milk.

Dad had mischievously eased the boat toward the buoy that marked the west point of Eagle Island and was amused at Blackie's interest in the bright red and white wooden marker poking three feet or so above the surface of the water.

"Blackie must have some hunting dog in him," he remarked. "Now he looks like a dog on point." The boys and Dad were watching him intently. Mother and I were just as intent on balancing the food on our laps.

Active all day, we kids were always hungry and would have had bites of sandwich in our mouths by this time had we not been taught to wait for the blessing. No other boats were in sight. The only whisper of sound came from the movement of the boat as we slipped through the water. Blackie cautiously stretched his muzzle forward to smell the buoy when suddenly this THING, this Monster of the Deep, whacked against the prow of the canoe just under his nose with a resounding bang.

Blackie leaped. He twisted in the air over our heads and crashed into the relative safety of our overloaded laps. Mother and I ducked reflexively, and the boys subdued Blackie in one smooth motion. The boat merely shuddered, then steadied. After a dazed moment, we laughed. Dad lifted the dog over the boys' heads and settled him at his feet behind the thwart, and Mother with a mildly disapproving look at her husband salvaged some of the sandwiches and fruit. We munched as we journeyed home. The spilled milk made its presence felt in other ways, but I remember our hilarity as we washed out the launch cushions—with Blackie's help—at our evening swim.

It wasn't easy to part with Blackie at summer's end. Tearful protests were in vain. I felt like a hypocrite when

I sat on the dock hugging him and declaring I would never forget him and making wild promises for the next summer, while he in his ignorance squirmed and tried to get me to play. Our request had been granted, but only for the summer. We had made a bargain; we had given our word. Somehow our parents made us understand that we swam in the summer, went barefoot in the summer, had pets in the summer; in the fall we returned to city ways and shoes and school.

Eventually I accepted it. No doubt the fact that we had never had a pet in town helped. Getting back to our neighborhood friends and the schedule and rhythm and stimulation of school and church was absorbing. I did not fully experience the loss until the first weekend trip back to the island to finish closing the cottage. There I found myself listening for Blackie's mad circling around the house, expecting his irrepressible greeting whenever I stepped out the door, finding our family swim incomplete with one merry member missing.

We all softened the blow by picturing the next summer, when we assumed we could again have the companionship of a dog and kitten. I don't know about my brothers, but I vaguely saw Blackie himself waiting all winter at the dog pound until he could be a part of our family again. I thought of him as a child away at school for the winter; summer would surely bring him home to the island. The boys planned for other dogs other summers, but for me there was only Blackie.

Painful Parting, Joyous Reunion

"YOU CAN'T FIND ME!" Everett's shrill, exultant singsong sounded. In truth, for a moment I couldn't. From the looks of things, the sloping side yard might have been harboring a stalled sailboat race. Clotheslines strung at every possible angle among the trees were hung with a tablecloth and sheets. My parents were hurrying to get the wash done before the Eustises' annual outing for the ladies of their church the following day. My young brother's tanned bare feet finally showed below two white sheets. Silently I slipped closer and, with a yell of victory, pulled one sheet aside.

"Gotcha!"

Alas, the pins popped loose, and the wet sheet billowed to the ground. Too late I remembered Mother's warning not to touch the wet laundry for fear of smudging it.

We were out of sight of Dad, who might have rebuked us. We did not like to have him chide. He had been greatly concerned during the spring, for summer school classes in

German were not offered because of hostile feelings left over from the World War. We heard nothing of his financial worries until the problem was solved when Schilling Tours employed him for ten weeks as a tour manager for a luxurious ocean voyage and trip through Europe. His background in German history, literature, and music and his knowledge of the Romance languages made him an ideal guide.

The thought of separation must have been especially difficult for my mother, whom Dad always treated as if she were not only precious but also fragile. They were not demonstrative in front of us children, but more than once Dad spoke to us of his early romantic feeling for the lovely self-assured librarian whose skirts swished as she hastened about her duties. He was obviously proud of this strictly reared minister's daughter as she learned to dance, to ride the little surfboard we pulled behind the launch, to play tennis, to entertain friends under island conditions. They usually agreed in their opinions about books and plays. We seldom saw them disagree and never heard them raise their voices. They settled whatever differences they may have had out of earshot of their children. My father, like most of the husbands in our civil, proper community, made the decisions about where the family lived based on his career, but I am sure he always consulted Mother. Dad never projected the feeling that Mother was not capable; rather, he wanted to be able to take care of everything for his family himself.

For the moment, however, and several times in later years, there seemed to be no alternative to the forced separation.

It was good that he enjoyed the work, and he proved to be a popular tour manager. Mother never spoke of loneliness.

Unfortunately, that spring Dad had begun to suffer intermittent pain around his waist; the doctor later diagnosed it as shingles. At this time Dad did not know what it could be, and he definitely did not want Mother to talk about it. My father never complained about any illness, especially anything that limited him or made him dependent in any way. If he had done what he could to correct it, he would simply ignore it, as if it did not exist. When the sting of the tiny midges (or no-see-ums), which was merely annoying to the rest of us, caused his eyes to swell nearly shut, he wore a fine veil on a sun hat and continued to transplant bushes and care for the yard and garden as usual. I got the feeling that it was not quite acceptable to complain about hurts — and worse yet to cry.

I was vaguely aware that Dad would be traveling instead of teaching, but the two weeks before his departure seemed like forever in my mind. When our game of hide-and-seek among the laundered sheets got us into trouble, Dad was working at the open porch between us and the Eustises' cottage; Mother spied us from the window above the sink. She tapped on the glass and beckoned. Guiltily Everett and I started inside. We had to pass Dad to get to her. He was in his bathing suit — we all wore bathing suits on wash days — but he also wore tennis shoes and always the red bandanna tied around his head to keep the sweat out of his eyes. He vigorously pumped the short handle of the washing-machine agitator one way and then the other. We could hear the hot soapy suds swishing. He didn't look up.

We pussyfooted quietly along the porch, past Bob helping at the washtubs, and slipped inside the kitchen after stepping into the waiting bucket of water to rinse the grass and dirt off our feet.

"I'm sorry, Mom. I forgot," I mumbled. "I was chasing Ev, and I didn't mean to pull the sheet down."

"No, of course you didn't, Marjorie. Now come with me and bring the basket. Your father will have to put the sheet through the suds again. And you bring the pin bag, Everett, and clean off any pins that fell on the ground."

The space Dad was working in was constricted, for our cottage had originally been built on half a lot, and only a narrow path separated it from the Eustises' fence. Their cottage sat graciously in the middle of their sloping yard, while ours perched on the very lake edge of our lot. There

Our cottage faced the lake; the kitchen was added on to the back.

the kinnikinnick bushes covered the bank with green and brushed against the porch. On wash days our father carried two buckets along this path to the top of the steep bluff where the water-trolley windlass stood on its platform, crowded between the cottage and the fence. He fastened one pail to the wheeled trolley and released it to run down to the lake to fill. As it descended along a heavy wire, it unrolled a stout cord. Energetically he cranked the windlass, rewinding the cord and hauling the pail back to the platform, repeated the process for the second one, and carried the full buckets into the kitchen, where Mother heated the water in a small copper boiler on a three-burner kerosene stove. Dad then transferred the water to the square tub of the washing machine. The work was slow, and he was thorough.

Every fifteen minutes a new batch of shorts and shirts and towels and undies was declared clean. Dad fished the garments one at a time out of the hot suds with a stick whitened and smoothed by long use and fed them into a wringer. Wringers were also bracketed to the edges of tubs filled with cool water. Mother soused the clothes in the first tub to rinse out the soap. I was learning to crank the wringer for her but much preferred to help splash. Bob wrung them out of the second rinse into the heavy wicker basket (big enough that Ev could still cuddle into it), and Dad carried it to one of the clotheslines.

Almost everything we owned — except the bathing suits we were wearing — went into the washing machine, for we washed clothes only once a month. Dad's dress shirts for his trips to the university were pressed with flatirons

We looked like ragamuffins with Mother and Ev in homemade bathing suits and Bob and me in hand-me-downs.

heated on the stove and later with a gasoline iron that hissed and sputtered. Ernest Heilman, another professor, happened by on a wash day once and teased, "It looks as if the Myerses dress mostly in bath towels." It would have been hard to do anything in secret on Crane Island, but to have washing on the line on the Eustises' once-a-year party day would have been unforgivable.

Mrs. Eustis was a fine-looking grandmother, tall and sturdy with gray braids circling her head. I experienced her mostly as a voice — strong, sometimes imperious — calling her husband to his chores or giving him directions. Didn't he ever get tired of being told what to do? I wondered. We assumed he was quite deaf, for his wife's voice was often raised, but we noticed that when he and Dad talked about fishing he could hear just fine. He never complained.

All the wash, including every bath towel, was dry and tucked away before evening. Party day dawned bright and windless. That morning I had glimpsed Mr. Eustis's slender, slightly stooped figure, his gray hair covered as usual with an ancient straw hat. He had brought the Women's Society members the half mile from the landing at Zumbra Heights and handed them from boat to dock in his careful, attentive way. Mrs. Eustis stood at the head of the stairs, graciously greeting them and ushering them across the broad lawn to the deep breezy porch.

Now, while the ladies were busy after the noon meal, Mr. Eustis started the launch again, apparently heading to Zumbra Bay. I supposed he had been sent back on an errand. Not until early afternoon did I realize that something was amiss. I had been lying on the big bed on the screened porch, reading and noting the festivities next door.

Suddenly Mrs. Eustis's stentorian voice broke the stillness: "Benjamin, Bennjamiinnnn!"

In my private game, I counted how many times she called her husband's name before he answered.

Why not just call him Ben? I mused.

Mrs. Eustis finally appeared at the fence to ask my parents if they had seen her husband.

"Are the ladies going back so early?" my mother asked.

"No, not till four, but I promised them a ride around the island, and now Benjamin's not here."

"He must have misunderstood," my mother suggested. "You're always welcome to our little launch. I'm afraid it would not hold all your friends at once, but we could make two trips."

"No, no, no! It's his place to be here when he's needed."

Now anger was apparent in her tone, and I felt sympathy for him.

"Well, let us know if we can help."

Promptly at four, the long white motorboat pulled in at their dock. Mr. Eustis stepped out, and the ladies trooped down to be squired back to the mainland.

Several days later Dad descended the steps to the lake and noticed Mr. Eustis at his double dock partly hidden under the boat canopy. The old man had one foot on the dock and had pulled up a leg of his pants to examine his skin. Dad walked over to see if he was hurt.

Shamefacedly, Mr. Eustis twisted around to show the angry red blotches behind his knee: chigger bites. A row of red swellings also circled his waist.

Reluctantly, he confessed that the ladies' chatter finally got his goat, and he had fished on the far side of Eagle Island until the sun made him drowsy, and he went ashore for a nap. When he awoke, he congratulated himself on avoiding several hours of tedious talk, not realizing until a day or two later that the sand must have been alive with chiggers.

Later I overheard Dad elaborating on this story as he described it to Mother. He was amused at Mr. Eustis's fidgeting as he tried to ignore the intense itching. "He squirmed in his clothes, and every time I looked away he took a swipe. Finally he grinned and just gave up and dug in and enjoyed a good scratch."

"Poor man." Mother breathed softly. "Did you suggest Mentholatum to cool the bites?"

"Yes, but you know and I know that whatever he tries, he will do penance for a long time."

What did Dad mean when he said Mr. Eustis would "do penance"? Was God punishing him for slipping away? But God knew all our thoughts, didn't He? He would know that Mr. Eustis kept his promise — to be there at four. Mr. Eustis didn't know about the boat ride his wife had planned. She just expected him to be there every single minute to do exactly what she wanted, and he got tired of that. Rebelliously I thought that I would have left, too, even if God sent the chiggers afterward to bite me — though I couldn't quite believe He had done that on purpose.

For a while the conversations we heard across the fence were mostly Mrs. Eustis remonstrating, and Mr. Eustis did a lot of solitary fishing.

We used to have fun with the list of Crane Island Rules and Regulations, which hung on the back door. Usually the door stood open, hiding the big yellow placard. Over the years, I saw a change in how my law-abiding parents felt about these rules. Sometimes when friends from the Cities were visiting, Mother or Dad described the unusual history of the Crane Island Association, voicing their support for its aim to establish a place where people could live close to nature and in harmony with the teachings of their religion. But in later years, everyone laughed when the rules were exhibited and read aloud, for they seemed old-fashioned and overbearing, narrow-minded, really just plain fussy.

"There is to be no swimming on the Sabbath."

We Myerses broke this rule every week, although we swam discreetly and quietly at our own dock.

"No loud or boisterous noise after eleven P.M. or before six A.M."

That was not hard to obey, although the word "boisterous" always made me think of Mrs. Eustis — perhaps she helped write the Rules and Regulations. I always had the uncomfortable feeling that she did not quite approve of my brothers and me.

"No alcoholic beverages" was no hardship for us.

We also thoroughly approved the prohibition of commercial enterprise.

But "No use is to be made of the Association dock or rowboat or other property on a Sunday" seemed extreme. By this time many people played tennis on Sunday afternoons.

I was once told that one of the older ladies complained at an association meeting that a potential sale had been compromised when the couple had seen "tennis players in swimming attire" using the court on a Sunday. She felt that the community would soon become "rowdy like some places on Phelps Island." I had played tennis on a Sunday — often in a swimsuit. Did this make me a wicked person? Had I contributed to the tension on the island between the good people of the original church group, who had every right to set up rules to protect their wishes, and the new people? But the world was different now, wasn't it? Some people didn't even go to church on Sunday. Our family respected these older people and their beliefs, and their rules were not too onerous for us, but renters thought them quaint. To me it seemed only good sense to be ready for a cool dip in the lake after a tennis game.

That summer our family was separated for the first time. Dad made several trips to Minneapolis to confer with Schilling officials, and he wrote a flurry of business letters to make reservations and arrangements. Then he was gone. We young ones kept pestering Mother with questions about when we would hear from him, but she had received only a hasty postcard from New York City. Nine days was the length of the ocean crossing on the luxury liner. His itinerary was nailed up on the wall, and when friends stopped by, knowing Mother must be lonely, we gathered around it and tried to figure out how many days a letter would take to reach us on Crane Island.

When a letter finally came, what a treat it was. Written at leisure as Dad lay in his deck chair, it told of uniformed waiters bearing flaming baked Alaska high above their heads. There were movies, dancing parties, interesting people. Soon the letters came more rapidly, two at once to my brothers, and sometimes to me, Miggles. Dad told of an elaborate meal served in a fifteenth-century castle and a lazy afternoon on the Rhine River. He shared adventures, strange sights, and tales of the giddy young woman in his group who had already become engaged twice since leaving New York. He told of a black marble sunken bathtub in his private suite in Italy and of the woman who remembered Paris not for the Louvre but for a pheasant dinner at the hotel. Mother read the letters to us over and over. What must she have felt imagining the parties and her handsome young husband offering his courtesies to all the ladies for those nine weeks?

Our lives settled into the old routines and passed without incident. If the responsibilities seemed heavy to Mother,

The summer sun turned Bob and me a rich brown; Ev, like Mother, was always more fair.

she did not speak of it. The lake, of course, limited our activities. But this ring of protection against danger could itself be a danger — if we should disobey the rule never to go in a boat or swim without permission or we needed to get to a doctor in a hurry. But everything was tranquil.

In no time at all, it seemed, we were anticipating Dad's return. Once he was on the ocean, there was no way for him to mail letters, and he overtook word he sent from New York City. We knew only the approximate day of his return. Although Mother was fairly sure he could not be here so soon, she prepared a nice salad for lunch on Tuesday. When he did not come, she put on a banquet that evening. We all paraded to meet the boat but, alas, he was not there. Disappointed, we returned home, trying not to worry. Wednesday Mother gathered all the food she had left for a celebration at noon, but again we returned home without him. By suppertime we were sure he would be there, and Mother, having used up all her festive food, prepared pancakes and sausages. Again we ate a solemn, quiet meal without Dad. Groceries would be delivered on Thursday afternoon, and then we could prepare another feast for supper. Unable to give up what had become a habit, we all went to the north end of the island to meet the noon boat. All Mother had in the house to feed us after her three prodigious meals was cornmeal mush.

Arriving a few minutes early, we spotted the big boat emerging from under the White Bridge. Everett ran off to hunt turtles in the reeds; Bob and I stood at Mother's side sharing her anticipation but ready for yet another disappointment. As the boat left the narrow bridge and approached the markers in the bay, Bob cocked his head and looked at Mother.

"Do you hear something?" he asked, and he had his answer in the look of eagerness on her face. Involuntarily she stepped forward, and Everett came scampering back. As we all walked to the end of the Big Dock, we heard the powerful blast of the steam whistle on the smokestack. The captain and the purser, Dad's longtime friends, kept up the salute until the boat was docked. Other passengers obviously enjoyed watching the emotional reunion as we hugged, laughing and all talking at once. Dad grabbed Mother and whirled her around, then picked Ev and me up both at once for a bear hug. He saw that Bob had reached for his worn suitcase. Dad started to shake his son's hand, then proudly pulled him close for an embrace.

"Mother tells me you've been a real helper."

We children fairly dancing in excitement, the five of us began the trek back to the cottage.

Mother served the mush the way Dad liked it — sliced and fried in butter with clover honey — while I studied this dear person, so familiar yet now so strange and mysterious in his new role. And then he opened his suitcases. For Mother there was a fabulous bottle of her favorite Coty's Rose Perfume from the rue de Rivoli in Paris. Bob unwrapped a huge Gouda cheese covered with firm red paraffin that had been bought in Holland, while Ev opened a package containing a grinning nutcracker carved by the man who played Judas in the Passion Play at Oberammergau. Then Dad produced a small cylindrical jeweler's case and presented it to me. The only thing I could think of that would fit in that tiny box was a thimble — perhaps made of silver or gold, but still a thimble. And, oh dear, I supposed it was to encourage me in learning to sew, and I must act pleased. It was so good to have my daddy back, and I must not hurt his feelings.

What I found when I opened the pretty white box, coiled there in a cotton nest, was a slender sparkly silver chain, and at the end of it was a watch! Relieved and delighted, I reached my arms up for a hug and kiss.

"I saw it in the window of an elegant jewelry store called Bucherer's when I was in Switzerland," Dad explained, "and I knew right off this was the gift for you." He called it a bull's-eye watch. The small globe of solid glass showed the face of the watch on one side. If I tipped it a little sidewise, it distorted and magnified. If I turned the tiny globe clear around, I saw the shiny machinery that made the clock work — the little balance wheel, the gears, all were exposed to view. I knew I would always treasure it and often wear it.

We moved to the front porch and piled on the big bed around Dad while he told stories, foreign words sprinkled here and there to tease us and, of course, to teach us.

"Did they have lots of watches at Bu — Bu — what you said — that jewelry store, Daddy?"

"Oh, yes, I'm sure they did, but when I went in, a formally dressed man came to greet me and seated me at a glass counter. Then another gentleman brought just the one bull's-eye watch I pointed out in the window. He laid it in front of me on a velvet mat."

"Why is it called a bull's-eye?" Ev asked.

"A whole eye is really a globe just like that. We see only a small part of the whole human eye because it is hidden inside the skull. A bull's eye is bigger and rounder."

Dad took the little box from me and showed me how to wind the watch. He let each of us admire the moving parts. Then he described the main shopping street in Paris, where he had bought Mother's perfume, and told about the bicycles and the clothes the riders wore.

Soon we all scrambled to the kitchen, where Dad made a triangular cut in the heavy wax covering the cheese. We each had a tangy taste before it was tucked away.

Everett's gift prompted many stories about the close-knit little mountain town in Germany where the people lodged tourists in their homes during the play's once-a-decade run. In the intervening years they tried to live according to the biblical precepts of the play.

Dad's shingles improved during this happy time, but the relief was short-lived. Perhaps responding to the strain of reading and study in the school year that followed, the shingles progressed up the nerve to his left eye. In addition to the constant pain, his vision was temporarily seriously handicapped, and the doctors made numerous changes in his glasses. Mother spent many hours that winter reading aloud the answers to the essay examinations Dad always used.

I did not consciously worry about my father in the midst of the fun and busyness of the school year. To me, he was indestructible and equal to any emergency. He had found a new, exciting job when he needed it, hadn't he? And now, as summer approached, he was overcoming the shingles and again we looked forward to our blissful interlude on Crane Island.

Living Legends

MY PARENTS MET AT Northwestern University. When they married and moved to Oxford, Ohio, and then to Minneapolis, they left all their kin behind in the Chicago area—Dad's in Park Ridge, Mother's in Evanston. Thus we saw our relatives only on infrequent visits. All four of our grandparents—the youngest eighty-four—spent a week at Crane Island in the summer of 1920. It was a surprise to discover that our parents had once been children and that legends, as we perceived our grandparents, could look like regular people. I began to understand that Mother's family came from a line of scholars and ministers stretching back to England, while Dad had risen from the working class by his own efforts.

Grampy Myers was a favorite. He had visited us in Minneapolis, so we knew him best. The attentive, birdlike way he cocked his head when we talked bespoke his lively interest. One day he was sitting quietly in the living room with a group when suddenly he jumped up and paced the floor. Anxiously, Mother asked what was the matter. "I mustn't get stiff," he replied with convincing firmness. "I don't want anyone to have to wait on me." In the mornings we heard him softly counting to himself in his room as he marched in place, knees brought up as close to his chin as possible.

He was slight and unstooped, with deep-sunk eyes, and his thick, short-cropped hair was white like his mustache and the goatee that half covered his black bow tie. His morning table prayer always began "We thank Thee, Lord, for refreshing sleep," and I can still see his small white head bowed in what I took to be simple, unshakable faith. In those days I thought how strange it was to be thankful for sleep.

Dad told us many stories about his revered father's extra measure of service to others. As an army sergeant in the Civil War, he had been a friend to the men in his command, sharing food and supplies and laboring over letters to the families of two men who were seriously wounded. At his carpentering work, Grampy faithfully lived out his interpretations of biblical admonitions. When he visited us, he would not use the streetcar on Sunday because, he said, "the motorman and conductor should have a chance to worship and rest on the seventh day like the rest of us."

Somehow Mother managed to keep the four grandparents comfortable in our cottage with only one real bedroom. The stairway to the dormitory turned a corner. The stairwell was covered at the top with a hinged canvas door that remained closed in the daytime to keep the heat out of the downstairs. When the door was raised, it formed a divider of sorts between the double bed on one side and, on the other, the boys' big swinging bed, suspended from the sloping rafters. On each side, two large windows came clear to the floor; corners were curtained off to act as closets and to give some privacy.

The boys moved into my small bedroom, and our folks took me into their bed, as they had when I had whooping cough. My parents slept on the big bed at the end of the front porch, where they heard the lapping of the waves and the moonlight glimmered through the elm branches. If it rained, they loosed great canvas curtains, which unrolled behind restraining wires. If the wind blew, the canvases flapped noisily but kept the water out.

A snapshot of the nine of us by the front porch shows Bob and me, both deeply tanned, crouching in the front. That dark tan and my love of the water explain why Grandfather Olin Mattison, a distinguished, scholarly looking Methodist minister, called me "little Minnehaha" in his loving, precise way. In the picture, he stands in the back with Grampy and is almost as tall and slender as my father. His daughter, my mother, stands next to him. She was named for him and all her life had to explain that she was Olinia, not Olivia. Because of her small size and unassuming attitude, she was often called Linnet, and later Lynn.

The two grandmothers sit in the middle row with chubby, blond Everett, head cocked sideways and squinting against the sun, squeezed between them. They were so different. My mother's mother, Annis Donkersley Mattison, was small like Mother, delicate yet indomitable-

All of us posed in our Sunday best during my grandparents' visit to the island in the summer of 1920.

looking in her filmy flowered dress. She sits drawn to her full height, unruffled, genteel, her hands idle for once without her tatting shuttle. As a minister's wife, she was frequently "at home" to callers, Mother told us, while her eldest daughter, Auntie Myrtle, helped supervise the six younger children. I felt shy of her frail appearance and composed manner and remained at a wistful distance. I many times glimpsed her sitting in a stiff chair on the front porch observing the view and tatting. When I proudly wore my

Sunday dress with the tatted medallions and yards of edging, I thought of her and behaved with utmost care.

Mary Cutler Myers, in contrast, was taller, heavier, sober, quiet. From the time Dad first left the little lattice-porched cottage in Park Ridge, he wrote to her every Sunday afternoon. She seemed very proper, but during their visit to the island Dad teased her into admitting that she had always wanted to go fishing. He promptly taught her how to troll with a casting rod and rowed while she fished for hours. We all rejoiced when she caught a scrappy three-pound largemouth bass, which he helped her to land with a gaff hook. In the snapshot he took that day, she looks at the camera with her lips parted in a proud, bemused half-smile.

I always felt a little uncomfortable with this grandmother. She seemed weary somehow, unresponsive, and I hoped I would not be like that when I grew old. She often let her mouth hang open a bit, and I was aware that I did, too, since my encounter with the heavy swing board. There was some talk of a mildly deviated nasal septum, but no action was indicated. Whenever Mother saw me breathing through my mouth, she whispered in German to spare me embarrassment, "Mund zu!" I strove diligently to conquer the habit and thought a little resentfully of Grandmother Myers. Had I inherited this habit from her? I wasn't sure why my daddy wanted to spend so much time with her.

On Sunday morning this grandmother mixed a custard for ice cream. Dad brought out the old wooden bucket with its hand crank and the sack of rock salt. He put a generous block of ice into a gunnysack and pounded it into

Grandmother Myers and her three-pound bass

small chunks with the side of his ax. He fit the chunks into the bucket around the two-quart container that Grandma Myers had filled three-quarters full with her mixture. He cautiously sprinkled salt on each layer of ice and kept a clean cloth ready to wipe the salt away before opening the container lest it contaminate our treat.

Grandfather Mattison, serious and reverent at our Sunday-morning prayer service, now insisted on turning the crank.

When we circled past the back porch to check on the ice cream's progress, he tried to convince us that if we did not show up promptly when the wooden dashers were removed, he would have to do all the licking and tasting by himself. We didn't quite believe him but kept a close watch to be safe. He did in fact share the tasting and pronounced the ice cream very good indeed.

Only one helper, Grampy, showed up besides us children when Grandma's bass was prepared. Dad took it in a bucket of water to the fish stump halfway down the hill toward the garden. A beautiful shower of iridescent scales followed the metal scaler, which Dad applied vigorously. Then, in shorter strokes, he scraped around the underside and tail. Some of the scales attached themselves willy-nilly to even the most fastidious of the watchers. Grampy skillfully filleted the fish, using the hand that had lost a thumb in a carpentering accident, and we had a chance to stare in wonder, unreproved. Bob dug a hole for the bones with the garden pitchfork and his bare feet. Dad scraped the slime and truant scales from the fillets with the back of his knife, then washed them again and placed them in a clean basin. Mother repeated the process in the house, then offered the men a pan of water with a few drops of Lysol added to take away the fishy smell. Grandmother Myers looked proud that evening at dinner when we each enjoyed a portion of her catch, crisp and delicately browned.

The Myerses stayed after the Mattisons left so Grampy could help Dad raise a dormer at the head of the stairs. The space—barely large enough for a cot—had small windows on three sides. I decided I liked having a grandfather who was a carpenter. Although he seemed diminutive to be my tall daddy's father, he really knew how to do things. I felt great respect for Grampy and was impressed that he was teaching my father; until then, I had thought my father knew everything. I discovered that the new dormer was a wonderful place to sleep occasionally. Looking out over the front porch roof to the lake, I dreamed myself into the world of the birds and soared fearlessly through the leafy branches and over the water.

As Dad started to town one day, his father caught him alone and with great circumspection handed him his big gold pocket watch.

"It's not keeping time, Walter. Can you leave it with a jeweler for me?"

In answer to Dad's questioning look, he added distantly and with dignity, "It fell into the lake. Must have got some water inside, I should think."

Grampy had planned things well. Dad had to run for the boat and could not take more time for questions. Finally, just before the Myerses left, he confessed like a guilty child. He had been fishing from the rowboat without success. Having decided to move to a new place and forgetting his son's warnings and his own earnest promise, he stood to pull up the anchor. Suddenly, he found himself in the deep water. Grandfather could not swim. Fortunately, he had kept hold of the anchor rope and managed to pull himself back into the boat. He stayed out in the sunshine until his clothing dried and told no one. I believe the whole experience was never revealed to Grandma, who was inclined to worry — evidently with good cause. Thus I discovered that Grampy could be sly about his shortcomings, although for so many years he had been held up as an impossibly perfect model.

During the Civil War, Grampy had kept a diary that revealed his agony of spirit when he volunteered for the conflict, which, as a good Christian, he hated — but he felt he must support President Lincoln to help end slavery. He shot "toward the enemy lines" because it was his duty, but he never chose a man "as target" for the bullet. When he himself was shot in the thigh, the bullet fortunately passed between the bone and the tendons; on the field a man probed the wound with his fingers to be sure the bullet had come out the other side. After recuperating in a hospital, Grampy was furloughed home, then later rejoined his regiment. He was discharged at war's end as a first lieutenant.

Although his wound entitled him to a pension, he would not accept it. "All risked their lives. What more could anyone do?" he said. He returned to his meager income from painting and carpentry. When he was forty-four and his wound began to cause him pain and slowed him up at his work, Grandmother persuaded him to request the pension, which began at four dollars a month, then increased to six dollars; finally, at age ninety-four, he received one hundred dollars per month.

I saw my grandparents in the rosy glow of my parents' affection. Understanding that I was expected to try to be like them put a burden of "goodness" on my shoulders. Also, I began to realize I did not want to be just like anyone else — or to live just to please someone else. I wanted to find my own way, even if it made me different, even if that made me feel a little lonely sometimes.

While the relatives were there, I often hung around the kitchen with the women, trying to be helpful. Meals might have been a burden, but Mother knew the fish Dad caught fresh almost every day always brought delight: pickerel, with its white flesh and strange forked bones; firm, dry bass prepared with a delicate coat of cornmeal; crappies; the sweet sunfish Mother sometimes pickled, bones and all. Potatoes were boiled in their jackets, straight from the garden, and occasionally served in a buttery cream sauce with parsley. With sliced tomatoes and string beans or peas and a dish of applesauce, she had an easy meal that everyone praised.

The grandmothers liked to help, and I enjoyed being the one who could show them where everything was kept in the cupboards. I went ahead to the porch to set the tables. Dad had made two from an old piano crate and covered them with white oilcloth. Then he hinged them to the front wall of the porch so they were out of the way until we swung them up into position. There we ate, all facing the lake except for the two who sat at the ends.

Mother presented the food on the motley collection of plates and dishes she found on the shelves when we acquired the cottage. There was some willowware and some fine hand-painted china, and each of us had a favorite plate. Milk and ice water were offered, with coffee for the adults and occasionally lemonade on a hot afternoon. Mother made no pretense of serving elegantly, even when we had guests. At her call, each of us carried a family-style dish from the kitchen through the living room to the front porch. Because things cooled quickly in the fresh air, the blessing was the only formality unless Dad was carving.

When our little family was alone again, the pace of our activities slowed. Mother asked me one noon to wash the dishes while she caught up on writing letters. I stood before the large blue enameled pan of warm suds in the kitchen. I heard my brothers playing at the dock; they had finished burying the garbage and digging angleworms for the bait bucket. It was hot, and for a fleeting moment I felt betrayed, then forgot my annoyance as I sloshed my arms to the elbows in the slippery suds. The china and glasses felt smooth, almost soft to my caressing touch. The silver pieces slithered easily through my fingers and splashed back into the pan. I played with the little metal dipper that carried the cream from the neck of the milk bottle, and I closed its sliding cover. I scrubbed the dipper with a bristly black bottle brush on a long metal handle. I did not hurry. The juice from the garden beets stained the soapsuds, and I stirred them briskly with a small mesh basket on a handle that held discarded slivers of soap that otherwise would have been wasted. I stirred vigorously until the tiny bubbles multiplied into a foaming pink mass like cotton candy.

The window over the sink looked out on a large elderberry bush enlivened with clusters of small red berries. The wren who lived there strutted on the branch, tail perpendicular, wings aflutter for balance. Her throat vibrated to the unexpectedly coarse, loud song that came from her tiny body.

A bit of lemon sherbet lingered in the sauce dish I had used, and I licked the tangy sweetness. I had put off to the last cleaning the chimney of the hanging lamp from the living room. When Mother pulled the lamp down to light it, the pearly blue dimpled globe rode on its chain up toward the ceiling. Its light was sufficient for our games of rummy and Old Maid. This morning she had clipped the wick and set the slender, slightly smoky chimney aside until we had hot water. Now I wiped it with paper napkins and took fresh water to make suds to shine it. I heard the song of a Baltimore oriole, turned quickly, and caught the flash of his orange breast. From a distance came the call of a male cardinal — confident, insistent.

From the front porch came my mother's voice: "Marjorie, what *are* you doing out in the kitchen so long?"

"Washing the dishes, Mom, like you said."

Mother's chores, too, rested lightly upon her. Her quiet, unassuming hospitality made visitors feel comfortable. Perhaps it was that we enjoyed the place as it was and made no pretense and no apology. Mother had meals ready regularly, but we were not on a rigid schedule the way we had to be in town.

Dad came in later than we expected from fishing one day after the grandparents had all left, and we delayed our noon meal for him. Mother was reading us a story on the porch and simply continued without comment. We watched him walk back and forth, unwinding his fish line to dry on the inconspicuous nails driven for that purpose high along the house wall of the porch. He put the rod and reel in place above them and carried his paddle to the wall bracket in the living room.

As Mother continued to read, he came and listened for a while, then rolled up a newspaper to form a megaphone. Pointing it away from us, he spoke into it in a pathetic voice: "I want something to eat. Please give me something to eat." Softly at first, then circling the megaphone toward us: "I want something to EAT! GIVE ME something to EAT!" While he kept us entertained and wanting to try it ourselves, Mother, laughing, slipped out to the kitchen to rewarm our lunch and put it on the table.

If the floor began to look untidy, she had us all don bathing suits and go outside to play. She too would put on her bathing suit—and take off her glasses. Her hair and her smooth forehead were covered by a bathing cap. Garbed thus, she mopped herself out of the house, and we all went for a swim—the only other thing I can remember her doing without her glasses.

When Dad was at the university, Mother had some precious hours to herself, which she rarely had during the busy school year as a faculty wife. When she entertained in town, she used the Haviland china and placed her real lace doilies under tall crystal sherbets for her celebrated Date Delight dessert. Sometimes she let us children wait on table while she chatted easily with her guests. She wore her dark hair in a coil around her head when she dressed up, and a long silky dress made her look taller and so dignified. I could see that Dad was proud of her, but it was not her appearance that prompted him to urge me to pray to be like her, but rather her patience, her honesty, her quiet serenity, her steady faith.

Here at the lake, this former librarian always had a book — fiction, religion, philosophy, or popular astronomy — at her elbow, and I wanted to live like that, too. Sometimes, under her direction, we lay back in the canoe or on the lawn and identified the Pleiades, the Big Dipper and Little Dipper, the Milky Way, or Mars in the night sky.

One memorable evening late that summer of the grandparents' visit, Mother and I put launch cushions and bed pillows in the canoe and paddled out onto the lake. We drifted with the breezes all night. To me it was a daring undertaking. I felt exposed, aware of possible dangers of lake and sky, away from the cozy enclosure of the cottage and all the family. It was unfamiliar to have Mother in the position of the strong protector; we usually looked to Dad for that. I thought of Grampy and wondered vaguely if the world looked dangerous to him as his strength slowly faded. He never complained but only expressed gratitude for each day his Maker granted him, as he put it, and for the "energy of mind and soul to meet it."

We woke at early dawn, chilly and wet from the dew and aground on the mainland shore. The first rays of light burned away the stars and announced the coming dawn as Minnehaha and her mother paddled home.

Pirates

IN THE EARLY DAYS, herons occupied Crane Island unchallenged, for fishermen and mainland neighbors feared the great birds. In nesting season, heron parents kept a fierce watch from the branches of the tall hardwoods. The cormorants — smaller, blacker, bolder — also seemed menacing with their glinting yellow eyes, their bullet-straight flight on rapidly beating wings. It was rumored, we were told, that anyone who set foot on the island risked being attacked and having his eyes pecked out. The grisly details whipped up our imaginations, and my brothers and I tried to discover where we could have hidden to spy on the threatening creatures had we been here then. We began to think of ourselves as pirates: fearless, cunning, seeking a place to hide treasure and plan dangerous adventures.

Thus began the reign of the Pirate Gang. We developed a special interest in the icehouse, built in the bald spot in

The Pirate Gang at rest

the island's center. It was opened two or three times a week when the caretaker made his rounds. He dug out a new section of the darkly shining ice and neatly chopped away several chunks. Then he took down heavy iron tongs, selected a piece, grappled it out, and swung it into a wheelbarrow, where he brushed it clean with a broom. The ice had been cut from the lake the previous winter, sledged up the hill with a team of horses, and packed in insulating layers of spongy sawdust.

Late one summer we pirates decided to hold our yearly midnight feast there at the dark of the moon. For a moment when my alarm clock dinged at the appointed hour, I could not understand why. Grateful for the skimpy light from the stars, I searched the dark, then heard the squeak of ropes as my brothers stirred in the swinging bed upstairs. I listened for our parents, asleep on the wide front porch.

No sound. I slipped out of bed and into my shorts and shirt and pulled a package from its hiding place under my dresser. With it and my flashlight I tiptoed out of the cottage.

My brothers were already waiting on the narrow back path, but nothing seemed familiar in the gloom. Even my bare feet, so used to this path, hesitated. Bob quickly covered my flashlight, and the darkness contracted even closer. Gradually my eyes adjusted, and I tiptoed on the clammy grass, following my brothers' shadowy figures across the Commons. The cheerless, windowless icehouse loomed in the darkness. Bob fumbled with the door fastener. Echoes of scary games of kick-the-can, when every shadow, every whisper of sound was full of danger, assailed me anew, and I peered around in the threatening darkness. The door opened grudgingly, impeded by a pile of sawdust. A damp smell, acrid but not unpleasant, met our nostrils.

The darkness was even more intense than it was outside. The pale beam from my flashlight showed the vague outline of stairlike shelves where the caretaker had cut out chunks of ice in layers. Cautiously we explored and climbed up three levels, kneeling in the soft cool material. Either the light or our clumsy progress disturbed the bats. Unconsciously, although we knew better, we ducked our heads. As we selected a place to sit, my foot touched a sliver of ice. A lizard? A snake? I stood huddled on one foot with all my toes curled under and turned to see Everett contentedly digging in the soft wood pulp to make a fort. My brothers and I climbed to the top level of the ice. We clustered there quietly to let the bats return to their roosts or slip outside.

At last we heard the sound we were waiting for: the wide, heavy door creaked open a crack and then a little more to let tall, slender Betty slip inside. She was followed by pretty, easygoing Dort, who for once was not lagging. Two years older than Bob, the Harris twins were lively companions, full of ideas. They shut the door, then softly whispered, "Red dagger pirates."

We sang out in unison "Blood, blood, blood," only to have Betty shush us. The girls did not immediately climb up to join us. When I turned my flashlight on their pale faces, they hissed, "Wait, we have to be sure we're not being followed. We heard funny sounds."

"What kind of sounds?" I was ashamed that my voice squeaked.

"Very strange. We couldn't hear them much. It could have been an animal. Does a fox ever trail humans?" Betty rasped. "You know the caretaker said he saw one on the island when he came out here on the ice."

When I thought of a fox with its sharp teeth and quick claws, I wished I'd worn my pants and sneakers. My bare legs sprouted goose bumps.

"Oh, a fox would hide," Bob scoffed.

"C'mon up here and tell us about it," I whispered, wanting all the company I could get.

"Wait." Betty turned toward the door. "I hear it again, kind of a brushing sound. Maybe a person. A fisherman could have come in at the North End through the reeds and no one would have seen him. Maybe . . . " Betty muttered softly.

"Why would he follow us kids?" Bob interrupted. "That's nonsense." Ev and I moved closer to him in the darkness.

I shone the light around again. Even Bob looked apprehensively at the corners of the icehouse. A stranger was something we seldom thought about. No one had ever come to the island without an invitation.

Soon Betty and Dort relinquished their fears enough to make their way across the damp sawdust toward the banks of covered ice. They asked us to turn the light on them and began to climb up. The bats flew around again. We Myers kids held our breath, for the girls were frightened of them. The twins were watching their slippery footing and at first did not notice. When Dort stopped to empty her shoes of sawdust, a bat swooped across the shaft of light. The girls both shrieked. Bob slid down to them and handed their packages, which they had dropped, up to Ev and me. He boosted the girls up to where we had packed the sawdust in a little circle and set down our treats. Dort kept looking over her shoulder and refused to sit until the flashlight was propped up in front of her.

A long, square, blood-red railroad spike leaped from Bob's hands into the center of the group as he murmured, "Red dagger pirates." Our private dagger, decorated with a huge metal nut and two painstaking coats of bright red paint, symbolized evil deeds.

"Blood, blood, blood," we intoned, the flashlight making spooky shadows. Then, chilly in the scary dark, we unwrapped our feast. My Fig Newtons looked delicious, but I wished I had packed something less sweet. They were pounced on happily enough, along with the fudge the Harrises made, the kind I liked best, with walnuts. As Bob and Betty got to arguing about bats and whether they deliberately tried to hide in a woman's hair, I remembered the potato chips. I had tucked the package into a pocket, and they looked crumbled as I retrieved them and dumped them onto a paper plate. Ev and I munched on them anyway and told about how Mother and Dad chased occasional bats out of the cottage with tennis rackets.

As we slipped home, I saw fiery red fox eyes glowing behind every bush and tree. After plunging my feet into the bucket of water beside the back porch door, I tiptoed to my room. Not stopping to change my clothes, I jumped hurriedly into bed. I pulled my feet up quickly, cleverly eluding any foxes or real pirates who might be lurking in the shadows of my bedroom. I said my prayers again and cuddled down to sleep.

The Pirate Gang flourished in the years the Harris girls and the Innes boys were on the island. The last time the gang planned a midnight feast, I stayed overnight with the Harris twins, who with their mother rented the big Tyler cottage that year. That summer my brothers and the Innes boys — Bob, who was my age, Donnie, almost as young as Everett, and John, who had had polio — were to join us at midnight to go to the gravel pit, where we would consume in unholy, piratic secrecy the candy and cookies we had prepared. None of the boys showed up. We girls shuttled from window to window, peering out into the dark, sure that they would not oversleep and fail us.

Presently Mrs. Harris came out of her bedroom wrapped in a white cotton housecoat and began to recite a ditty that she made up as she went along:

> The lady pirates paced the deck
> whence all but them had fled.
> One lady pirate muttered, "Heck,
> The boys are still in bed."

When she teased us, her small dark eyes danced in her broad face, and her short, heavy body shook with laughter, but the truth is we depended on her for ideas. Stories this good lady told inspired the pirates on many occasions. Bob read pirate stories voraciously and readily supplied details about scuttled ships and unlucky seamen forced to walk the plank.

Our first pirate den was in the bushes at Our Point. Bob cut away branches in the dense growth and whitewashed stones to outline the little room, which could only be reached by crawling through a passageway in the brush. Another secret hiding place was underneath our cottage, where Bob had to remove a section of the cross-lathing to admit us. The space was cluttered with rowboat oars, a discarded sail for the canoe, and a chair that needed a new caned seat. To get there we moved in a squatting crawl over a soft, shifting dirt floor.

The first real problem we encountered was persuading the Harris twins that the field mice had better places to nest and that all the cobwebs were empty. Dort looked back and shuddered. A hairy spider with a fat black body was wedged into a corner of the flooring above our heads. Since the girls had already moved past that spot, we convinced them to hunker down. Bob reached under a two-by-four and located the railway spike. All our eyes were on it as Bob drove it into the ground at the center of our little circle.

Our voices were serious, too, as we intoned our incantation, for we knew what was to follow. We were all going to select a vein in our wrists. I watched appalled as Bob led the way. I had filched the needle from Mother's sewing basket and carefully dipped it in rubbing alcohol, as I had seen my parents do when they dug out splinters. My anxiety increased as each one in turn added a drop of blood to the end of the dagger. Now I was the only one left. Determined to be brave, I jabbed and missed the vein and had to prick again. Mixing those drops sealed our union.

That was difficult for me. I was timid about hurting myself, and I felt an unsettling thrill of disobedience in deliberately injuring my body, even so slightly, against all our parents' teachings.

One year a would-be pirate summered on the island. A big boy who had no one his age to pal with hung around us whenever he got a chance. Grant was nice enough looking but awkward physically and easygoing — content when he could follow us little kids around. If we let Grant into our games, his clumsiness spoiled the fun. With the unfailing cruelty of children toward one who is different, we did our best to avoid him. If we saw him coming, we ran away and hid. His parents encouraged him to keep busy at home, but when he could elude them, he followed us—uncomplaining, compliant, but always a misfit. Telling him we were bad pirates only encouraged him. We attempted to frighten him by exaggerating the tale of our bloody initiation, but nothing daunted him. He wanted to be a pirate, too. We tried to think of some experience short of walking the plank that would scare him away.

The bluffs on the island were a constant challenge to my brothers. At a tender age, Everett rigged a cardboard body onto his coaster wagon. On the hood of his "car," he ensconced my cat. With Snowball contentedly purring—"like a smoothly running engine," Ev said later—he kicked off on the path beyond our garden in a rattling, bouncing, bone-jarring trip to the bottom. The cardboard box flew off first, and Snowball was close behind, but Ev reached the bottom delighted with himself.

Later, when the toolshed near the Hermanns' cottage was renovated, a couple of baby buggies were discarded, and Bob took charge of cutting them down until they were merely frames with wheels. The boys on the island then risked scratches, spills, and bruises in daredevil races—first down the milder slopes, then on the steep overgrown ones on the North End.

In the shed of the house the Harrises rented again that summer, the twins also found a discarded baby carriage. The wicker was discolored and broken in places, but the wheels still worked. Why not scoot Grant down the steep bluff in the baby carriage? they thought. They assembled the pirates to consider their plan, and agreement was instant. But could we stuff him into it? Would he agree to it? Would he think it was an initiation? Would the buggy even hold together?

We needed a test run. The Harris house was next to the Big Dock, but the high hill in front was not cultivated. Small bushes and vines and trees volunteered in the grass. We fell to with a will. The girls and I cleared out the old magazines and boxes that had been stored in the buggy. The boys oiled the wheels. We all trailed along as Bob took the buggy out to the bluff, aimed carefully, and pushed it over. It bounced and teetered, then slowed halfway down as it caught on a kinnikinnick bush and tipped gently onto its side. Perfect! Jubilant, we retrieved the buggy. Our dress rehearsal was definitely a success.

Early the next afternoon we gathered at the Harrises'. The island was quiet, drowsing in the heat. The previous night I had tried to imagine taking that ride down the bluff myself, and now I was experiencing some doubts, which I anxiously shared with the older ones.

"What if he falls out?" I fretted.

"Huh, if we can squeeze him in, he'll be lucky if he can ever get out," someone answered.

"Well, the buggy tipped over, you know, on our trial run." I was still unsure.

Now everyone spoke at once: "Oh, it's OK." "Stop worrying." "He's tough." "Don't spoil things."

Then Dort spoke up. "Wait. Maybe Marj is right. Listen. It could be bad . . ."

Suddenly I felt disappointed. Had I talked them out of the whole idea? Now I wanted to try it. Excitement that I had held in check before seized me. I almost convinced myself Grant would be OK. He was big and tough. Anyway, my brothers did this all the time with their cut-down buggies.

Just then I looked up and saw Grant himself wandering through the gate dressed in a long-sleeved checkered shirt and dark green pants. That's what he'd been wearing the day he sat at the top of our stairway to the lake. Dad was wrestling with the launch he'd been working on so long, now trying for the first time to start the engine. Again and again Dad turned that brutally heavy crank. Again and again the engine failed to catch. Each time, Grant roared in mocking laughter, "Har, har, har!" How could anyone treat our beloved father so?

That memory clinched it. All at once I didn't care what happened. This buggy ride was meant to be.

When the boys and the twins told Grant to climb into the buggy, he did not question them. He must have assumed this was his initiation. He did not even glance at the hill. I was outwardly calm as I held the buggy steady while the boys made a stirrup with their hands to help him up into the cab. The sunshade had to be folded back out of the way. Grant's head and shoulders stuck out— arms loose, long legs hanging over the end. He had a happy grin on his face.

I wasn't worried either. I had yielded to a tingling sense of adventure, cutting loose from all my inhibitions. Now I'd find out what would happen.

And so we pushed the buggy to the edge of the bank. Suddenly it looked much steeper than before, and again I began to have qualms. Grant was still not concerned: he looked foolishly happy, even waving to us and kicking his long legs.

Should we try to stop him? It was now or never!

The buggy wavered on the edge for just a moment, then it was gone. It plunged so fast it took my breath away. I shivered with excitement. With Grant's weight, it gained speed and wobbled crazily. It caught on a vine and nearly capsized. It bounced back and sideswiped a small bush.

"Hey! Stop me. I want out!" Grant yelled, but by then he could do nothing about it, and neither could we. The carriage careened crazily and crashed over a willowy bush, its branches whipping wildly and slowing the runaway vehicle. Then again the buggy seemed to leap ahead.

"Gosh!" I heard someone gasp.

Otherwise we watched in breathless silence, helpless terror building. Grant's arms and legs were flailing, but the buggy was still upright. Bouncing and now nearly flying, it burst through the weeds, dug into the narrow stretch of sand on the shore, and stopped at last at the water's edge.

I could hear no sound. I saw no motion. Had he fainted? Had a heart attack? Was he — maybe — dead? Terrified, I scrambled down the bank with the others.

Thank goodness, Grant was unhurt. But Grant had had enough. He was wedged in so tight we couldn't lift him out. His face was blank, expressionless, as if a mask had dropped over it. Bob and the Innes boys managed to flop the buggy onto its side. We girls pulled on Grant's legs till he was able to wriggle loose. He lay there a moment, then staggered to his feet and, dripping, began to work his way up the bank. He stumbled along a little way, then stopped, turned, and gazed at us as we stood there gaping and staring stupidly at him. The look he gave us — frightened, helpless, beaten — I will never forget. Without a word he turned again and made his way on up the hill.

Apparently he kept his humiliation to himself. We were punished only by the guilt that was forced deep into our consciences by his disillusioned expression.

Our parents gave us almost complete liberty on the island. When we were younger, Dad had marked our names on our dock at the spots where we could have stood with heads above water. We respected their specific rules, yet somehow we convinced ourselves that our parents never knew of our later unsteady ascent into the branches of the coffee tree that overhung the tennis court and our experiments there with cigarettes. We began with corn silk wrapped in toilet paper but later found a pack of English Ovals that tasted barely better and made us dizzy. The fact that we knew our parents would disapprove made it attractive. The fact that they had not specifically forbidden it got it past our censors.

Once we set up another daytime pirate adventure. To make it secret and mysterious, we went to the island's wild North End, past the croquet wickets and the miniature golf holes on the Commons to where there were no cottages and the grasses and underbrush grew up around the trees. We followed in each other's footsteps to make the walking easier. Bob was leading, and then came the twins, the Innes boys, Everett, and me behind him at the end. Bob led us farther than we had ever been before. Bushes and weeds came up to our shoulders, and finally we slid down to the muddy flats. There occasional reeds appeared, and in the shallow water they grew profusely. Hollow and as dark green as bulrushes, they had brown tufts that graced the tips some four feet above the water and formed a dense whispering wall far out from shore.

Suddenly, an agonized yelp.

"I stepped on something. I'm stuck," Ev wailed.

A narrow rotted plank overgrown with moss was hidden in the sludge. A nail protruding from it had apparently penetrated deep into Everett's heel.

I knelt to look and grasped his ankle. When I pulled gingerly, the plank stirred in the gooey muck, but his foot did not come loose. I was frightened. Sometimes we imitated lockjaw with wild grimaces in our games. Islanders kept their lawns cleaned to protect barefoot kids and swimmers. Oh, why had we left the safe area?

The others picked their way back and gathered around us. While I balanced Ev, Bob pulled the plank away from Ev's foot.

"Does it hurt, Ev?" Dort hovered, sympathetic.

"It's hardly bleeding," Betty commented. "Maybe it isn't too deep."

But Bob pointed to a complete footprint on the mossy plank.

"He mustn't get dirt into it," I said, immediately anxious when anyone was hurt. Bob and I made a chair of our interlocking arms and carried Ev out of the reeds. He now was feeling no pain and thoroughly enjoyed his ride. As soon as we reached familiar territory, the other pirates slipped off to their homes.

Dad couldn't believe our story of the imprint. He examined Ev's heel and saw only the tiny prick. He sent us back for the evidence. Scared and eager to convince Dad of the severity of our little brother's wound, Bob and I ran the length of the island. Bob remembered just where we had entered the brush, and we quickly located our tracks in the reeds. The plank came out of the viscous muck with a sucking sound. We carried it between us at a jog trot, long-faced, penitent, frightened. By the time we arrived bearing the plank, Dad needed no further evidence, for he had found another tiny hole under the ankle bone. The nail had penetrated between the heel bones. He managed somehow to probe from each direction with cotton swabs carrying a mild solution of iodine to cleanse the wound.

The small wound healed, and the scar faded even as the pirates' enthusiasm for adventure subsided or was channeled into pursuit of more conventional thrills.

Dance of the Raccoons and Dance of the Heavens

"YOU LOOK PRETTY, MOM. I wish I had hair like yours." I must have been seven or eight. She had dressed in a ruffled, knee-length party dress and arranged her brown hair in ringlets that spread over her shoulders and chest.

One other time Mother had dressed as a little girl for a party at the Perines' on Enchanted Island. She enjoyed being seen as a younger woman and always was secretive about her age — perhaps because she was three years older than Dad. Her hair had no hint of gray, and her skin was the softest in the world. One of the games that night was to guess ages, and surely Mother should be forgiven for her pride in the fact that the guess closest to her age was three years too young.

Now she was ready for one of the Edholms' lively costume parties. Camilla Edholm had recently made the rounds, inviting everyone on the island to the festivities. Camilla's blue eyes shone steady and confident under her

How I admired the ringlets Mother wore for a costume party.

thick, gleaming yellow hair, bobbed and brushed back in simple bouffant style. Her firm chin gave an impression of quiet inner strength, but her cheeks dimpled when she smiled, and her full figure indicated that she enjoyed good food. Her gracious manner and readiness to share interests made her many friends.

She and her imposing, deep-chested, husky-voiced mother lived in an apartment on the East River in New York City. Camilla taught English literature in a high school on Long Island, and her mother lectured across the country as the executive secretary of a national health organization. They had traveled all over the world together — to Kashmir, to Europe, to visit the White Indians of Darien. They and my parents enjoyed sharing tales of their travels. I felt my safe little island crack open, and the whole world began to beckon to me wherever I turned. It was almost unthinkable, but someday I would not have my parents with me.

They had once been without me, and sometime I would be without them. Maybe then I would travel—perhaps even alone.

The Edholms' comfortable front porch boasted mementos from all over the world, including a fine collection of Victrola records. On one a tenor voice sang "How lovely are the messengers that sing us the gospel of peace." Mrs. Edholm, or K.R.J., as she called herself, told us the words were, "How lovely are the messengers that sit on the dove tail of peace." She watched us with a smug expression, and her eyes danced mischievously. Forever after, that is the only way we could hear the words, and we wondered what strange kind of bird this could be. It was also the first time we had ever heard anything approaching irreverence for a religious song. She enjoyed our confusion hugely.

Another record we always begged for was Ernest Thompson Seton recounting the story "Three Sioux Scouts" about surviving dangers by signaling each other with the rasping "rr rr rr" of the she-fox, the haunting voice of a hoot owl, and piping bird calls. We kids and sometimes the adults practiced rendezvousing with each other using our amateur imitations of those forest sounds. Ev was the best at this.

Tonight as we approached the Edholms' porch, Japanese lanterns sent out welcoming beams of flickering colored light, and we could smell candles. We youngsters were to be allowed to stay up to observe at the party for a short while; we would return home to bed when the dancing started. We eagerly awaited our parents' dramatic entrance. Dad, who was known as the best waltzer in the faculty dancing club, dressed as a pirate with a patch over one eye and a knife between his teeth. He carried Mother over his shoulder, her head and curls hanging down his back. Shrieks of laughter met them. I jumped up and down and clapped with the shepherdesses and ghosts, woodsmen and dancing girls in tutus. For a few moments the boys and I basked in their glory, then tried to melt into the crowd. But Camilla came toward us dressed in a colorful South American peasant skirt and blouse and offered cookies for us to eat on the way home. We had turned toward the door when, over the din of voices, we heard a loud clatter.

"Another guest," Bob said hopefully. "Wait a minute. Let's see."

Mrs. Edholm was moving grandly through the crowd announcing, "We've a show for you. Come to the windows."

It had grown dark as the group gathered, and now she trained a flashlight on the bushes at the top of the bluff, where the contents of a basket had spilled: on the grass lay two pie tins and a set of sleigh bells, nuts, seeds, eggs — one of them broken — apple parings, and vegetables.

A large dark animal with thick fur moved deliberately across the lawn, poked its pointed nose into the food, and reached delicately for tidbits with small purposeful paws.

"The raccoon hasn't been here for her handout for quite a while," said Mrs. Edholm, "but we're ready for her. We're glad she came back to show off for you."

Some of the guests had brought flashlights and were shining them around in the bushes.

"The basket is rigged on a wire that goes to that tree," K.R.J. continued. "When the coon touches the wire, the basket crashes down, and the tins and bells alert us that she is after her food."

In the shrubbery, two bright eyes showed up, and then two more, and two more. Three babies with their bandit masks and ringed tails barely showing had followed their mother and now moved in to share her feast.

"So that's what you've been up to, you naughty girl!" K.R.J. cried. "See, the lights don't bother the babies, either."

The guests had made room for us children at the center window, and I peeked in on this tender scene, as I supposed, of a happy family. To my horror, I saw the mother, who was still stuffing herself, lumber across the little hoard of food and bat her slender babies out of the way before they could even taste anything. She returned to her feeding. The babies hesitated, tried again, got cuffed harder, then drew back and waited. But for naught. Mother raccoon finished up the food and picked her way back across the yard with the pitiful babies, tails dragging, following meekly. Was this possible? A mother who treated her babies this way?

I had sentimentally imagined that in nature mothers sacrificed everything for their young. Dad had told us stories of a bird that pretended to have a broken wing, risking her own life to draw attention away from her nest on the ground when danger threatened. I felt embarrassed for this unfeeling raccoon and tried to think up excuses. Perhaps the babies were not old enough for this kind of food. Didn't the mother always know best? And where was the father? Everyone I knew had two parents.

Several years later, another dance was held on that porch, and I did not have to leave early. My partner was my brother

Bob. I dressed in a hiker's outfit with heavy boots, and he as a barefoot Indian. I took it as a compliment to my dancing that he trusted me so close to his bare toes. I was impressed that he moved so rhythmically and gracefully — no wonder he could play the banjo in a band. With his inspired lead, we danced steps we had never danced before. Hope flickered that someday I would be an acceptable or even a sought-after partner floating in some handsome fellow's arms.

Just as Camilla was everyone's favorite, K.R.J. was everyone's authority. Mother took me to talk to her when I, entering puberty, felt I should be wearing a brassiere (or a "pimple ring" as my friend Ruth's envious little sister called it). Mrs. Edholm's air of complete knowledge helped Mother persuade me that I would be safe in delaying that grown-up garment for a bit. I was agonizingly shy and blushed constantly, too embarrassed to take any part in the discussion. I was relieved when it was over and felt resentful and diminished somehow — not, I think, because my maidenly development was discounted, but because what was happening to me was so special and so private I could hardly share it, even with my own mother.

This advice was given on Mrs. Edholm's back porch. She stood on the step above me, her eyes amused in her otherwise solemn face. She wore her thick, nearly black hair in braids piled on top of her head. Her hair had grown so long that she could sit on it, she bragged. She once confessed to worrying that people would think it was a wig and often casually pulled a strand loose when she knew people were watching her to prove it was not. In the winters, when Camilla was teaching, Mrs. Edholm did detailed, meticulous metalwork on trays and jewelry, which I found quite beautiful. Her most precious possession, however, was Camilla, and we rejoiced that she shared her daughter with us. Camilla's frequent beaux seemed not to be so fortunate.

Everyone loved Camilla. I'm sure we were not the only ones who marveled that she had never married. Infrequently she made a reference to a former romance or to letters or visits from men friends, but the consensus was that K.R.J. liked things just the way they were — with her attractive daughter drawing friends and attention wherever they went. I noticed that when my mother entertained, she stayed modestly in the background, highlighting her guests and their talents, but at the Edholms', K.R.J. was always center stage managing things.

It is hard to put into words what the Edholms' coming to Crane Island meant to all of us. They were in the forefront, endorsing and encouraging every improvement from resurfacing the tennis court to providing a community pump for drinking water, banding trees to control the inchworms, planting new trees, and clearing underbrush. They planned costume parties, amateur plays, all-island picnics that drew people together. They came at a time when the older clique from the Bethlehem Presbyterian Church was losing influence to younger, more pleasure-oriented ones, and the Edholms graciously helped the Myerses and others in efforts to lessen the tension.

Both of the Edholms were skilled in storytelling and in conversation — Camilla especially. She was only about fifteen years older than I — about halfway between my age and my parents'. We all enjoyed many evenings together, admiring the sunset from their porch or the rising of the moon from ours. Years when her mother did not make the trip to the island, Camilla was almost like one of our family. Whatever we did, there was always stimulating talk that stirred my young dreams. If only I could know what Camilla knew, remember everything Camilla told about travel in other countries — then maybe sometime I too could do these wonderful, fulfilling things that Camilla did and see the wide world on my own.

One evening I felt lucky to sit next to her when the family all set out in the canoe. She began to tell of going to Panama for a year as an exchange teacher. She joined a nature club, which entitled her to a trip to Barro Colorado, the mountaintop that became an island when the Chagres River was dammed to form the Panama Canal. Naturalists got a rare opportunity for study when the animals escaped the rising waters by climbing the highest mountain and were permanently isolated there by the deep water. They occupied three levels: colorful, screeching birds in the treetops, monkeys swinging and howling in the lower branches, and, among the creatures running below, bands of dangerous wild peccaries. The native guide, who spoke only a few words of English, ferried Camilla and several Spanish-speaking people across the lake in a large, tippy dugout canoe, armed only with a large machete. They disembarked on the rough shore and followed him into the brush, then up — and up and up — to the top. There they were finally allowed to rest on a log, but not until the guide had banged on it to be sure no snakes or scorpions were hiding there.

"Weren't you scared?" I interrupted.

"I was scared every step of the way. I was last in the single file" — she laughed ruefully — "and the man ahead of me could hardly get his feet out of his footsteps before I had mine in them. And I was looking over my shoulder whenever I heard things in the brush. There was an intermittent, weird, howling racket."

"Did you see the wild peccaries?" Bob burst out. He was excited. "I've read about their killing a hunter in Texas."

"You're right, Bob. Thank goodness we didn't see them, but twice we heard them snuffling and grunting. I don't know what we would have done if they'd attacked us. We picked our way down again and climbed back into the canoe."

"What a relief it must have been to get there safely," Mother breathed.

But Dad broke in. "Didn't you say there were crocodiles in those waters?"

"I knew you'd remember that, Walter." Camilla laughed and tossed her head. "Perhaps the trip back was the most dangerous of all."

She turned to us children and explained. "When Gatun Lake was flooded, the waters covered acres of big hardwood trees. Many trees near the shore were only partly covered, and crooked, dead branches stuck up ready to upset the boat — and, yes, we had observed some crocs on the way over. Now it was dark and hard to see our way. I was the only one with a flashlight — my Crane Island training, I guess—so I was elected to flash it around ahead of the dugout to locate the tin cans the guide had turned upside down over twigs and branches to indicate the best route. Sometimes we saw glowing red eyes and knew the crocodiles were waiting."

Camilla was not an English literature teacher for nothing. She knew how to tell a story and make it stick in your mind forever.

Parties were unusual on Crane Island, but one summer when some young faculty couples—the Dickinsons, the Hartshorns, the Cummingses—rented there, friends of theirs who played in the Minneapolis Symphony Orchestra, as it was then known, frequently visited them. They entertained us one evening by playing a familiar symphony without instruments but with motions and human voice. The drums beat assiduously, the violins tremoloed, and the piccolos tinkled against the steady "zum, zum, zum" of the cello players, who leaned forward and spread their legs to accommodate invisible instruments they belabored with imaginary bows against nonexistent strings. I was astonished to recognize a symphony I had heard with my father one Sunday afternoon under the baton of Henri Verbrugghen.

Canoe rides were frequently the highlight of the day. The west side of the island had the sunsets, we had to admit (although it also had the bad storms), but the moon rose on our side (and we seldom had winds stronger than a pleasant breeze). In the evening, especially when the sunset was lovely or the moon was full, we often set out in the canoe with a portable phonograph and some light opera. Soon the Edholms' or the Harrises' canoe might join us, and we drifted and visited, holding on to the gunwales of each other's boats so we would stay together. We carried flashlights to protect ourselves in the unlikely event that a motorboat might appear but otherwise gave ourselves up to the night.

The beauty of those evenings must have made a deep impression on me, for in a box of old letters I later found this attempt to describe them. It was written in a childish hand on ruled tablet paper.

MOONLIGHT THREE MOODS

I

The moon emerged from its rosy bed of clouds
Horizon mists increased its broad expanse.
As our frail craft moved toward it on a crimson path
An island's trees enticed it to their lacy web
And there it hung — a lantern huge and gaudy.
The whispering leaves wove patterns on its ruddy face
And branches reached to catch the moon in their embrace.

II

The moon shook off the trailing clouds of mist
And shone majestic high above the bay
The water was transformed to tiny glinting lights
That laughed and danced, and overflowed between the points
Of land that stretched so black and silent there.
The breezes wafted us along the sparkling way.
We rode straight toward the moon across the golden bay.

III

The breeze died down. The water ceased to lap
With soothing sound. The moon swung low,

An orb of silver just above the distant trees.
It cut across the water like a shining knife,
And was a deeper mystery than the gloom.
Like gleaming mercury, a path of pure delight
It lay — inviting, beckoning, laughing at the night.

One evening I shall never forget. It must have been late in the season, for we were still at dinner when we noticed an unusual amount of color in the eastern sky. We watched for a bit, and the colors unaccountably brightened. Used as we had become to observing only faint echoes of the sunsets, we were curious and hurried to the dock while ever more intense rose and orange spread across our sky.

Dad quickly packed us all into the canoe and paddled to the North End and out into the open water. The lake was not just calm; it was velvety still. We spoke in whispers, sensing that we were in the presence of a miracle. A roseate glow emanated from the sky. In the west apricot and yellow pulsed, and the clouds — puffy and still — were rimmed in bright gold. Then the intensity increased and vivid streaks streamed out. To the east, as we gazed in astonishment, the changing colors completely saturated and filled the sky until it was like an inverted bowl of glowing, glorious color perfectly mirrored in the lake.

As I looked down, the still water reflecting the color suddenly dissolved and disappeared. There was no surface. A strange feeling came over me. I saw the whole bowl of the sky reflected below me, and I was suspended, weightless, in the center of a globe of fluctuating color. I floated, transported, into an unreal element — neither sky nor water.

The illusion lasted for only a few incredible moments, and then the Edholms' canoe emerged from the west side of the island. Boats streamed onto the lake from other islands and the mainland. Some people stood on their docks. There was no sound, no calling of greetings. A sense of reverence held us in silence.

The colors eventually faded, but we continued to gaze about, then reluctantly we returned to a world that for me would never be the same. Ever after I would have a sense of the mystical, the magical, of the possibility of floating free of reality enveloped in shimmering beauty.

Raindrops and Teardrops

"LOOKS LIKE A DAY for fishing," Dad commented at breakfast as he dug his spoon deep into a bowl of oatmeal and cream. He looked out at the dark surface of the lake, where squalls scudded about and a lowering sky closed in.

"Still, you never can tell," he continued. "Remember that wonderful school of crappies I told you about—over at Zumbra? That was a sunny, bright day! And when—"

"Was that when the rich man's driver was having so much fun—" Bob broke in.

"Catching them one after another and couldn't quit?" Ev added.

"Right. He had his chauffeur's uniform on—and it was past time to pick up his employer. But he just couldn't make himself stop. I stood for a few minutes watching him; he no sooner dropped his line in than he'd hook another beauty. He'd look at me and say—"

"Just one more fish!" we all chimed in together.

Dad looked at Mother, and they laughed aloud.

"Sounds as if I must have told that story a good many times already," Dad said sheepishly. "That reminds me. We need a fresh supply of minnows. Anyone care to help?"

Three volunteers jumped up from the table, then with a glance at Mother turned back to carry our dishes through the living room to the kitchen before running to make our beds.

"Better put on your swimsuits," she called after us. "You'll want your clothes nice and dry if we have to stay in the house all day."

While Dad went to the toolshed for the big net, Bob looked under the house for the minnow bucket; its inside container was perforated like a colander, and its narrow top opened with a hinged cover. He swung it by its handle as we ran barefoot toward Our Point.

"Remember not to step into the water till I come!" Dad called after us. He didn't want our splashing to frighten away the minnows.

Unrolling the fine-meshed net attached at each end to a six-foot bamboo pole, Dad stepped quietly into the lake and walked out ten feet to waist-deep water. Bob held the other pole and stayed near shore as they slowly moved the net forward. Meantime, Ev and I were stationed a hundred feet away in the shallow water. We began to walk toward the net, splashing very little at first and more and more vigorously as we came closer. Soon we saw a flurry of tiny flashing streaks in a swiftly moving cluster.

"Keep the net tight down to the bottom, Son, or they'll escape underneath!"

Swooping together, Dad and Bob closed the net as they rushed onto shore. I held the bucket open while they poured the slippery creatures in. Ev gently picked up the ones that flopped onto the sand or were caught in the mesh. As we worked, the skies darkened.

Dad pointed toward Eagle Island. "Look at the lake — it's jumping like popcorn!"

And so it was. In an uneven, swiftly advancing line that extended as far as we could see, the lake continued to darken. A shimmering curtain of rain that seemed to be made of silver needles was moving toward us. The angry drops attacked the still surface, advanced up the shore, and drenched us. The torrents moved beyond us and to the trees and were gone. Water dripped from the leaves onto the grass, and near the boles of the trees the ground was dry.

Bob held one pole of the net upright while Dad rolled his pole, pulling Bob toward him. Then they hurried toward the house, Everett insisting on carrying the minnow bucket, now full of water and alive with minnows, a few precious "shiners" with their silvery sides among them.

"Come along, Marjorie," Dad called, for I was still gazing at the lake trying to understand what I had seen. I had never thought about a rainstorm having edges in terms of distance — only of time. It rained or it stopped.

After we got home, Dad busied himself with fishing gear, and Mother sat down at the sewing machine with her mending. We children were restless and got out some games but couldn't seem to settle down to a rainy day so early in the morning.

Ev thought of the big corner closets in the upstairs dormitory, and when Bob and I heard him rummaging around up there we tagged along and were soon involved in a spur-of-the-moment play about the Mohicans of upper New York State. In no time Bob had us deep in the tales of James Fenimore Cooper, and the bedspread became a tent. The drowsy sound of a steady rain on the sloping roof made us think of the moccasined feet of Indians slipping through the grass.

I was willing to leave Cooper's books to Bob, but I read anything else that came to hand, from Mother's little red leatherbound volumes of Shakespeare to Poe. After lunch I was ready to return to the brave endurance in Gene Stratton-Porter's *Girl of the Limberlost*, about a girl at home in a swamp in Indiana, when the Harris twins, Betty and Dort, appeared at the back door huddled under a single umbrella, a game of charades on their minds.

Unless the weather was really vicious, islanders seldom stayed inside. Sometimes dignified Professor Mudgett turned up in his rainy-day sweater with a hole in the elbow and a long strand of gray yarn hanging loose. I remember Professor Mudgett and Professor Heilman arriving at our kitchen door barefoot, with old coats held over their heads. Mother teased them about stepping into our "foot pail" before she let them in, and they replied that she would have to step in with them. It came to me as a surprise, but I realized that men as well as women found Mother attractive. She was somebody besides being my mother.

One time when a group had gathered on our front porch, Professor Heilman excused himself for a trip to the privy. On his return, having seen our large supply of toilet paper stored there on hangers, he remarked, "It looks as if the Myerses expect it to be a long summer!"

I couldn't understand why everyone laughed, and no one offered to explain.

But on this day, as sometimes happened when that need arose, the path was muddy and the rain heavy, and we girls retired to the little bedroom to use the "thunderjug," a heavy ceramic pot with a soundproofing crocheted "husher."

Betty and I perched on the edge of the bed as we waited to take our turn, and she said, "I was surprised that you didn't come up with an answer on that last charade. You usually are so quick with words!"

I was stung. I had very much wanted to be first with the answer. Why did I care so much? I felt quick tears start to my eyes and turned away ashamed. But she had seen, and, remorseful, said, "Oh, I've hurt your feelings. I'm sorry."

In my deep chagrin, I muttered, "Oh no, no."

To ease my embarrassment, she said, "Maybe you were yawning, and it made your eyes wet. It does mine sometimes. I thought you were crying."

"Yes, maybe, maybe a yawn," I mumbled unhappily, allowing a lie to embed itself restlessly in my conscience.

Late in the afternoon, when the clouds were finally clearing, Dad went out in the rowboat to try his minnows. When we rowed for him, we fought the wind to hold the boat steady while he cast again and again, sailing his line in a great arc and dropping his red-and-white Basserino exactly where he intended. He was often rewarded with a beautiful pickerel or a spunky largemouth bass that leaped and splashed as it tried to loosen the wicked three-pronged hooks.

But today we and our friends made popcorn in the long-handled screen popper and took our bowls to the front porch. Sun shone through the trees. We were commenting on the long shadows they cast when Dorothy noticed Emerson Woodward's canoe approaching from the north. It was shorter than ours and slimmer. Its red paint reflected the sunshine, brilliant against the blue.

"He must be taking Helen for a ride again," Dort remarked as he approached the Dickson dock, three stops north of us.

"He's too far out for that dock," Bob commented. "But he's all dressed up for something."

Emerson was resplendent in white duck pants and actually sporting a tie with his trim pullover.

He paddled forcefully until he had positioned his canoe directly in front of the Dickson dock, but maybe twenty-five feet out from the end. With nothing to counterbalance his weight in the stern, the prow rode high. The reflection of its red splendor made a spectacular picture. Pretty, dark-eyed Helen was waiting on the dock in a white outfit and red scarf. Thrusting his paddle deep and to the back, Emerson swung the light craft dramatically, pivoting at the stern. Smoothly it whipped around—and up—and over! We gasped and jumped to our feet. Emerson disappeared underneath the canoe with hardly a splash, only to come up a moment later, blowing water from his mouth and coaxing a long trailing weed from his hair. I hoped Helen wasn't laughing, as we were from our safe distance.

That night, remembering and peering into the dark from my bed, I reflected that if tears of disappointment and embarrassment had welled in Emerson's eyes, the ducking in the lake would have covered them, and he would not have needed to pretend to a yawn.

"Socks," My Modest Brother

"THANKS, ALL YOU MYERSES, for a faculty picnic to beat all picnics."

"Did you see Betsy squealing and wading in her bare feet?"

"And the dean taking a picture of that tiny fish he was so proud of."

"And the tennis!" "And the canoe ride!"

"You must come again." Mother, Ev, and I stood on the dock as Dad helped the last of our guests pack themselves into the launch for the trip to Mound, where they had left their cars.

The Yellow Canaries' schedules didn't fit those of Dad's colleagues in the School of Business Administration, so they had made their own arrangements for transportation. Since ten o'clock that morning, Bob and Dad had ferried forty people across from Mound and Zumbra Heights. We had set up tables at the grassy plateau near the gravel pit, where steaks and wieners and burgers soon sizzled on a crude grill.

Shouts of encouragement to the horseshoes contestants continued during the meal of potato salad and fresh tomatoes, radishes, and cucumbers, with a choice of watermelon or ice cream and cake, coffee or lemonade.

Now we handed down bundles of food, dishes, and clothing as Dad helped our guests find places. Every seat was filled, and Bob, now twelve, stood in his best shorts and Sunday shirt ready to start the engine.

"You have the good flashlight, Robert? We'll be watching for you," Mother called.

Although he should be back with daylight to spare, carrying a flashlight was an inflexible rule, since the boat's lights left much to be desired. Bob nodded and set about priming the engine. It caught on the second try, and he couldn't restrain a proud smile as he cast off the rope, backed away from the dock, and chugged around the point and out of sight behind the island, friends still waving.

Dad had given permission for Bob to act as skipper so that he could help Mother clear up the cottage. He put his arm around her waist and thanked her for the happy day she had made possible for his colleagues and their families. They watched until their friends disappeared, then Dad pressed on with the next job.

"He'll be fine, Lynn. Don't worry. A little better than a half hour each way will bring him home well before dark. Now, Marjorie, will you be Mother's helper with the dishes? And I'll round up chairs and tables from the yard, and Everett can take a sack and pick up the paper plates. Right, Everett?"

We tackled our tasks, and soon it was time for bed and a story. A delightful character Dad had invented — a Poppaloochi — was our favorite. Though I felt much too grown up for this, we nevertheless sang our Poppaloochi song.

> Hootchi, hootchi, hootchi-kootchi.
> I'm a happy Poppaloochi.
> I look healthy, fat, and fair,
> But really I'm just made of air.
> I'll come to play
> If you just say
> Hootchi, hootchi, hootchi-kootchi.

We were well acquainted with this boy who looked and acted like any other boy but was really made of air. You could put a hand right through him. Of course, this meant he weighed nothing at all, and one day he took advantage of his weightlessness when he jumped high to pick a lovely red apple. He aimed carelessly and missed the apple. He reached for the next branch to stop himself but could not grasp it. He found that he was floating off into space. It felt good until he began to realize nothing at all would be there to stop him. Soon he noticed that the apple tree and the house where his mother was waiting for him looked very small. After a long time, when he was getting worried and also growing hungry, an airplane appeared in the distance. It came closer, and there was a great noise and a whirling feeling. The boy became entangled in the propeller, and a kindly pilot pulled him inside and took him back to his mother.

However exciting Dad's fanciful stories became, a loving mother was always waiting to make everything all right again. Everett was asleep by the time the story ended, but I begged to sit up to see if Bob had come home yet.

"You'll hear the engine when Bob gets here, Miggles. Now cuddle in here and get your rest so you'll be ready for a happy day tomorrow."

"Please, I'm so hot. Can I have a cold sprinkle?"

Sometimes when the evening was breathless Dad brought a little pan of water at bedtime. We understood that the last drink of water and our evening prayers must be taken care of before the sprinkle. Then, in delicious anticipation, we awaited a tiny shower of coolness as he dipped his fingertips and snapped them once or twice. The rule was to lie very still afterward, and any faint breeze would renew the delightful refreshing sensation.

"Not tonight, Marjorie. It's not that hot, really, and you know that I always give each of you a cold sprinkle when I do one — and Everett is already asleep and needs to be tucked in. Why don't you settle down and listen for the engine?"

When my father talked about fairness, I knew I was beaten. Begging did no good at all. To be fair was the highest goal of parenthood, it seemed, and I had begun to understand that, although I was special to my father, I was no more special than my brothers.

I listened and listened for the boat, but I didn't hear anything except my parents' quiet voices as they sat on the front porch looking down at the lake in the twilight. I must have drifted off, because after a while I looked out my window and could barely see the pale patch of sky outlined by the darker trees. It was fully night. Where was my brother?

I slipped out to the front porch, where Dad sat with his arm around Mother. They weren't saying anything.

"Is he home?" I asked. "Where is Bob?"

Dad's other arm came around me, and I could tell he was worried, but all he said was, "He'll be along pretty soon now. Bob is so dependable. He's like an apprentice. He watches and uses his head and figures out how to do things."

"I'm glad he had that flashlight," our practical mother put in. "The one with the long adjustable beam."

"That's right, and I'm sure he will remember to focus it on the silver maple tree by the dock. He helped me plant that tree, you know, and there's still enough breeze to turn the leaves over and let the light reflect on the silvery side."

I couldn't tell whether my father was talking to himself or to us. We fell silent. Our eyes searched the great void of darkness that was neither sky nor water.

A shooting star cut an arc across the sky, and I watched it in wonder. I roused at length, realizing that I had been leaning half asleep against my father. I sat up and again strained to make my eyes see into the darkness. Then we heard it—a voice calling. It came from away out there somewhere. It was Bob's voice, but we couldn't hear a boat.

"Hey Mom, Dad, I'm out here. I'm coming."

Dad snatched another flashlight, and we all hurried across the lawn and down the steps to shine the beam onto the dock. Soon we could hear splashes but no boat: Bob was swimming. Gradually he emerged out of the water clad only in his underpants and socks.

He had got the guests safely to their car, but on the way home the launch had acted up. After trying everything he knew to coax it to start again, he had pulled it up on the beach and tied it to a tree on Hardscrabble Point. Then, carrying one of the long seat cushions stuffed with cork, he walked along the shore a couple of miles to the meadow opposite Crane Island. He left his clothes in a little pile with a stone on top, walked out into the lake, and began to swim, riding the cushion. He never has been able to explain why modesty required that he wear his socks to swim the quarter of a mile across the lake alone in the dark.

We climbed the stairs. Then Mother and Dad walked up the slope with Bob between them. They didn't seem to mind that he was dripping all over them. They questioned him about the boat's behavior and how he had secured it on the shore. They praised him for taking the cushion as a life preserver. Of course he remembered to take the cushion, I thought to myself as I followed along behind; they told us often enough. Poor Bob, he was already shivering a little in the night air.

How self-reliant he always managed to be, whatever the circumstances! I remembered how he practiced "Drink to Me Only with Thine Eyes" on the piano all last summer — both hands — until he earned the dollar Mother had promised him. With Sterno, he made engines for his toys. He took apart the cabinet phonograph and kept it, as well as the portable one, in working order. How come I never distinguished myself? Maybe I was too comfortable, too ready to be taken care of.

Dad decided to reward Bob with the overnight trip to Wawatasso he had been begging for. This special expedition was to be a "men only" adventure, including Everett. They planned a bonfire to cook wieners and marshmallows and would sleep in a pup tent on a tarpaulin with a tan army blanket to put over them. Mother and I were quite content to stay at home, and we contributed mosquito repellent as a farewell gift. They insisted afterward that they had enjoyed their outing, had even managed to sleep some, but we wondered about that when they were all so willing to go to bed early the next evening. One minute I felt lucky that I had stayed at home — Mother had played the piano for me — but the next minute I felt hurt that I had not even been invited. I found myself smiling as I watched them pick off wood ticks. It served them right.

A couple of summers later, Bob figured out how to put together a crystal radio set that crackled, protested, and finally pulled music right out of the air. He looked very wise as he sat concentrating on the little needle that made the contact, and he listened through his earphones. By 1924, he had added a big bowl to magnify and project the sound so that we could all hear a speech for the Coolidge presidential campaign. His accomplishments were marvelous to me, but not surprising, really. Self-reliant, thoughtful, alert to reports of new inventions, he was not easily dissuaded from his experiments. He liked to have Ev and me out of his way when he wanted to think. If Everett followed too closely, Bob swatted his hand in a glancing swipe across the top of Ev's head to enforce his boundaries.

When Ev in turn grew frustrated with Bob, he battered at him with his small fists. Bob simply held out his forearm and let Ev beat on it until he felt better.

Another of Bob's solitary pleasures was working with wood. From a big chunk of wood, he carved a shapely ship and fitted it with a jib, a mainsail, and a smaller pointed sail, the name of which I never knew. We all cheered when he floated it, and the wind filled those sails and carried it forward a few feet before a rogue breeze capsized it.

It seemed no time at all until he and Dad were making real sails for the canoe and rigged them to be hoisted up on the mast from the rear seat. They carved sideboards to be lowered, because the canoe's keel was inadequate to keep the sailing boat on course. We learned to wear bathing suits when we went for a ride, because it took a stiff wind to get the boat to skimming the water. Seated in the bottom,

Both Bob and Ev carved boats from chunks of wood.

we had to heed the call to duck below the reach of the sail's lower spar as the canoe tacked and the sail had to switch sides. Sometimes the boat went over, sail and all, and the fun was over until it dried out. Usually Dad took charge of the sailing, but Bob learned to do it, as he did everything. From the time he was a little boy, he apparently thought of himself as the responsible one. We still laugh at the tale of his going on an errand to Zenas Clark Dickinson's home, where he was greeted as Roberty-Bob. His voice was full of pride and scorn as he later fumed, "I'm not a baby! How'd he like it if I called him Zekety-Clark?"

When Dad was away at the university or on his European trips, Bob became the man of the house, watching out for Ev and me and sparing Mother what chores he could. Bob knew how proud his father was of him, but he began to think of Dad as a personification of authority. He would see Dad's muscular, square-fingered, all-capable hands as holding him back from taking decisive action on his own.

As he matured and began to need independence from our father, Bob became friendlier in demeanor, more outgoing — even astonished me by holding a door for me to precede him into the house. At the same time, he began to imitate our father's solicitude for us younger children, especially for my social development. Some time had to pass before I could see anything amusing in an event that took place when I was nearly twelve.

On a hot, still morning in July, Bob ostentatiously invited me to take a canoe ride with him. I was surprised. There was no wind — not even a breeze — to make a front seat paddler necessary. The sun was beating down. What a strange time to go for a jaunt in the canoe. Still, I had nothing else to do, and it was not yet time for our morning swim.

"Sure, where are we going?"

"Oh, nowhere. Just for a ride."

I looked at him, puzzled, but said nothing. Bob was energetic, but never just for the sake of being busy. He always had a purpose. When I was with him it was easy just to follow along. Although he was two and a half years older, Bob and I for years remained about equal in size. He and Ev apparently took after Mother, while I resembled my father; I reached five feet, five inches early, nearly catching up to Bob. He was much stronger, of course, and loved to do handstands and chin himself many times, could even grab a slender tree trunk and hold his skinny, muscular body horizontal to the ground, his broad shoulders bulging.

Now his straight hair, almost black, hung into his eyes as he leaned his head forward and started toward the lake.

"Come on!" he called, and I followed.

His awkward manner made me curious. I became even more curious when I discovered that he had arranged the lazyback and cushions in the canoe and indicated that I was to sit there. He paddled us around Our Point, where there were no cottages, and then let the canoe coast while he tucked his long paddle under the rear seat. He hesitated, grinning foolishly.

I finally broke the silence. "So far this is easy. Now what?"

Another awkward pause. He cleared his throat.

"Marj, you're getting to an age —"

Was this my reserved, uncommunicative brother?

"Uh, the boys will be coming around—"

What boys? What was he thinking?

"Well, when I go to these dances to play banjo, I see—"

What terrible thing that he couldn't put into words might he have seen at a dance?

"What, Bob? What are you trying to tell me?"

"Well, move over, will you?"

He eased forward in the drifting canoe, and I made room on the cushion beside me. He settled himself, and I waited. Again there was a painful pause.

I couldn't conceal my surprise when he clumsily put his arm around my bare shoulder, which was sticky with perspiration. We were not a demonstrative family, and I surely did not need to be made any warmer.

What in the world? Was he practicing on me, as he did when we practiced new dance steps? Had he met a girl he liked? He'd never said so.

Now he was talking again. Maybe I'd get a clue to what this was all about.

"Some guys get pretty aggressive when they're alone with a pretty girl. That good-looking new caretaker always has his eye on you."

Me? Pretty? With my skin so deeply tanned that my bright blue eyes seemed out of place, my brown curly hair carelessly caught back in a circle comb, and my old faded shorts with my long, skinny legs sticking out? And the caretaker? Yes, he was attractive, all right.

"Now, if you like the guy, this is OK," Bob declared, giving my slippery shoulder a squeeze, "but not on a first date. Not until you know him."

I could feel my cheeks flush. I had no overly eager boyfriends. My only experience was birthday parties and group dates at afternoon "sunlight" dances, as we called them. Romance was a hazy dream for the future. Was he making fun of me? Surely not. That wasn't like Bob.

"Oh, Bob, really! Come on." I couldn't see the need for a stuffy lecture on a breathless morning out in the middle of the lake. I was hot — and getting hotter — sitting here in the sun. I'd even forgotten to bring a sun hat. "I don't think I really need this. I don't even have a boyfriend. Let's forget it, can't we?"

But he wasn't finished. Bob was nothing if not thorough. He frowned a little, pursed his lips, and — horrors — I could feel his hand slipping down from my shoulder. Surely he wouldn't do this on purpose. But it couldn't be accidental. Whatever was he thinking of?

"But never let a fellow do this." Bob finished his lecture sanctimoniously as he touched my budding breast through my damp shirt.

I didn't know whether to laugh or cry. Suddenly I was mad. Nobody had the right to do this to me — not even Bob.

"Well, neither should you," I snapped, pushing him away. The canoe rocked dangerously. He didn't need to lecture me. I knew a thing or two myself.

My brother quickly regained his balance and moved back to the seat in the stern of the boat. His awkward manner fell away.

"Sorry, Little Sister. Just had to be sure Mother had got the message across."

All at once his effort to prepare me to protect my unthreatened innocence struck me as both funny and embarrassing, and I found myself giggling foolishly. Bob was obviously relieved, and soon we both began to laugh.

"I'm glad I won't be the guy who will try that on you some day. He's likely to get a ducking."

"Good enough for him." I was still a bit upset.

There was an uncomfortable pause.

"Well, today you overdid it, OK?"

His acknowledgment was a little grin. The experience left me with a comfortable feeling that Bob, like my parents, cared about me deeply, a feeling that blossomed when as young adults we both found ourselves in the helping profession of social work.

Swim!

"ME, MOM? ME SWIM the English Channel?"

A chubby ten-year-old, I stared open-mouthed at Mother as we and my brothers ate lunch at the table facing the lake.

"No, Marjorie, of course not. You could just try a long-distance swim from the island — maybe to Mound. That's two and half miles — much farther than you've ever swum."

"Mound takes a half-hour in the old launch, almost!" Bob seemed impressed for once.

"You recall when we all saw Annette Kellerman perform at the Orpheum Theater in Minneapolis?" Mother continued.

"And there was a seal!" Everett remembered, or thought he did. He'd only been six, but he'd heard a lot of talk about it since then.

"Yes, in a big glass tank on the stage," I added. "The seal was almost the same size as the swimmer." In the pool, her motions had seemed as fluid and sinuous as the animal's. I had delighted in their beauty, especially the incredible moving circle they made. The seal's black-whiskered nose followed the swimmer's toes; the woman's head — hair flowing — was close to the seal's tail.

"And Annette wore a black one-piece bathing suit like the one that got her arrested." Bob, at thirteen, was beginning to notice such things. The "shocking stocking," as the one-piece suit was called, was too daring back in 1907 when she first wore it on the beach.

He reached for another sandwich and helped himself to a tomato he had picked in the garden that morning.

"Maybe Marjorie would get arrested, too," he added cheerfully.

I ignored that but saw Mother give him a questioning look.

"Would you go with me, Mom?"

"Well, certainly. And we would follow all the rules for a long-distance swim. Dad would row the boat — and you'd be careful not even to bump against the boat, for then we'd have to disqualify you. I'd bring a candy bar to drop to you if you got hungry. We couldn't touch you. It would mean you'd be swimming for a long time, as Bob said."

"We're in the water all day long anyway. It would be fun!"

We knew about swimmers of the English Channel, for Dad had read to us accounts of the currents and waves and tides and bone-chilling cold. Last spring, inspired by one such news story, we dared each other — Dad, too — to

The Myers clan, lined up to dive from the barge

"duck ourselves clear under" the Minnetonka waters on the first day of May, just after the ice had gone out. A run to the house and my rough towel took care of my shivering and goose bumps, but the ache in my bones lingered. I had nothing but admiration for the brave Channel swimmers.

I'm sure Mother wanted to be the one to suggest the swim to me; that way she'd be certain I really wanted to try it and didn't do it just to please Dad. I could feel an eagerness in her to match what was building up in me. She was proud of her children's swimming skills, and I was excited to be chosen to try. Our parents often set up distance swims. Ev, at three and a half, had dog-paddled from the dock to the post anchoring the water trolley. Bob many times led processions from our dock to the swimming beach, and often we had dived from the rowboat and swum back to shore with Dad and Bob alternately pulling the boat along by its rope.

"It sounds great," I said enthusiastically, glad that now I would be the one trying a hard swim with my family helping.

"It's up to you, Marjorie." Mother was testing me again, but I had already made up my mind.

On an almost windless, bright Saturday morning, dressed in my hand-me-down gray cotton jersey swimsuit and with a heavy white rubber bathing cap strapped under my chin, I walked out into the water from the shallow side of Our Point across from the diving tower and barge on the east side. Dad and Mother waited in a rowboat supplied with chocolate bars and sandwiches and a Thermos of cold drinking water. Eight-year-old Everett squatted on the front seat dangling on a string the latest small sailing boat he had carved. Bob accompanied me.

Boats were essential in our life at Crane Island.

When the level of the tepid water reached my chin, we began to swim. Soon small waves developed, churning cooler water up to the surface. It was an invigorating sensation, and I got right into the spirit of the new game. Dad carefully pointed the boat, as he had promised, to indicate the shortest route across the big bay between Cedar Point on Phelps Island to the east and Hardscrabble Point, which like a skinny arm reached far out from the mainland to the west. If I ever reached that point, I knew I would be able to see my destination, Chapman's pavilion in the town of Mound. It seemed immeasurably far from the little rowboat.

Sobered, I kept swimming, the water a friendly, buoyant element caressing my body. But almost immediately I realized something was wrong. I couldn't settle into a rhythm. Bob had begun the ostentatious butterfly breaststroke he did so well. He sank below the surface of the water, then burst forth again, scattering spray in glittering arcs from his widespread arms. It was pretty to watch, but it spoiled my concentration. I tried harder, paying attention to the mechanics of my own stroke, but soon I heard Bob's teasing voice urging me to speed up. Not long after that he passed me a second time, making it obvious that he was swimming circles around me.

Bob was only slightly taller than I, muscular, and so lean he couldn't float. I habitually played — porpoise-diving, floating, changing strokes — and often fell behind when we did distance swimming. This time I was determined to be more businesslike and was disconcerted to have Bob outshine me from the start. This was my show, I thought, a bit resentfully, not his. Presently I saw him at the boat talking to our parents. Was he telling them I was too slow? No, he was hoisting himself into the boat. My, his arms were strong. I took my bearings again. I had barely settled into a steady stroke when I heard a splash. Bob had dived in again, and here he came—but toward me this time. Now I had the advantage.

"You're heading in the wrong direction!" I yelled at him.

"No, you are," he replied, trying to fool me. "See you tomorrow, Slowpoke."

I swam near the boat, only to have Mother warn me not to touch it. I began treading water while she explained, "Bob wants to go home. He'll be all right. We can watch until he reaches shore. He gets cold, you know, when he's not swimming hard. You'll have to set your own pace, Marjorie."

"Hmmmm, so I will."

I drained water out of my bathing cap and refastened the strap under my chin, then rolled to my left side to begin really to swim. The sidestroke was my favorite, and I began to put a good snap into closing the scissors kick. I stiffened all my muscles. There! It felt right this time. The water slithered by. I was an arrow, a javelin, slicing the water like a knife—holding the tension as long as possible to stretch the momentum. My left arm slowly pulled down while my right arm circled to position for the next strong stroke while my legs crooked wide, ready for their vigorous kick. Now stroke, power glide, coast—ready, stroke, power glide, coast—ready. Rest was part of the cycle in a steady rhythm. Breathing had cycles, too. Water sometimes broke over my cap and face as I stroked and exhaled. But I was ready for it and enjoyed the feeling of noisy immersion. My head was turned sideways to allow me to inhale slowly on the "ready" count.

I checked the boat at intervals, relying on Dad to line up the island and the shortest route to Mound. My confidence returned, and I hummed my "Night Cap" song in my mind over and over as the choppy waves rippled by. After what seemed like many miles, impressed with my progress, I approached the boat and called out "Time! No, I'm not hungry. What time is it?"

"Nine o'clock," came the reply.

I was appalled. Only an hour had passed since we started. It seemed as if I'd been swimming forever. I kicked hard to raise myself in the water and take stock. Phelps Island remained way in the distance, and I could still count all the windows in the Edholms' cottage back on Crane Island. Dad looked the teeniest bit restless, and I was humbled. It came over me again that I was the one this trip was all about. It was up to me to produce, and I'd surely not looked very good so far. My family had set aside a lot of time for me alone. They had not said I had to succeed; they had only said it would be fun to try. But I remembered the shiny look in my daddy's eyes when one of us got an A on a test at school and the time Bob got the blue ribbon at the hobby show with the phonograph he made himself. I was determined to speed up, and I switched to a crawl armstroke with a scissors kick (I never could sustain that flutter kick) and quickly ran out of breath and realized I had to have a plan.

Turning onto my back, I began a purposeful backstroke and imagined myself in a Channel swim. Icy currents would be buffeting me, cramping my muscles, sucking away my strength. I kicked, splashing rainbows of diamonds up against the flat blue sky away up there. How could anyone have it better than this? Swimming was just plain fun, and Mother's idea was proving to be great sport.

Cheered, rested, I settled down again into a sidestroke, and now it felt good — strong, rhythmic, effective. I remembered when Dad and we kids swam to Eagle Island: Everett finally had to get into the boat with Mother, but Bob made it all the way. Diving and coasting down to pockets of cooler water where Dad said springs fed the lake, I had gotten so far behind that Mother brought the boat back for me. But I made her let me finish the swim anyway, and they waited for me — patient and understanding, as always.

Stroke, power glide, coast — ready, stroke — keep the body stiff to hold the momentum. I had my second wind, and it was pure joy to have the lake all to myself and know I was making my way over the deep water, scaring away the fish with my vigorous splashing. I pretended I was all alone out here. The deeps had no terror for me after the drill Dad invented last year. Bob wanted to dive under the barge Dad had anchored at Our Point. One edge was in fairly shallow water, but the other extended over the twenty-foot drop-off. He had us practice holding our breath and swimming increasing distances under the water in our games. Then Dad tested us in swimming underwater parallel to the barge. When we finally satisfied him, we were allowed to dive under for real. All other activity stopped, and Dad was poised for a rescue if necessary. What a relief to come out to light and air again! What a feeling of accomplishment.

That was before Dad built the ten-foot diving tower on the point at the edge of the drop-off. Dad had taught me how to do a high dive with fists balled up, thumbs locked together, and arms stiff to make a shield to protect my head, but I had only once had the courage to try it from the dock

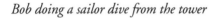

Bob doing a sailor dive from the tower

post. The games of follow-the-leader were my favorite. We tried new dives over and over — the potato splash, where we held our noses and jumped all doubled up; the swan, with arms outspread, toes together, and back arched; the jackknife, the sailor, the back dive, and the scary back jackknife. How is it the snapshops never looked as wonderful as we felt when we were sailing through the air?

A splashing up ahead caught my attention, and my folks were indeed signaling me. I looked around to check my position and thought I must be somewhere in Cook's Bay already. Everything looked unfamiliar. How could I have passed the long arm of Hardscrabble Point without realizing it? This swim was a snap after all. Then I realized I had inadvertently turned and headed toward Phelps Island instead of staying parallel to it. When I straightened out I could see Hardscrabble just where it belonged, reaching crookedly east from the mainland. A vast expanse of water still stretched between it and me. I would have to negotiate this before I even entered Cook's Bay. Two and a half miles was indeed a long way.

Mother noticed my dismay and held up a Hershey bar. They brought the boat close and dropped it to me.

"The shoreline looks different from down here," I apologized. I was surprised to hear Everett's voice. I had forgotten him.

"Can I have some candy, too?" He was eager. We seldom had candy unless Mother made penuche or fudge.

All of a sudden I was aware of how long they had all three been out in the hot sun on my account. Dad was busy with Ev and his little boat.

"Dip your hat in the water, Mom, and it will cool you off when you put it back on." I had forgotten that it was she who had taught me that trick. "Have you eaten your sandwiches?"

"No, not yet, Marjorie. It's only ten-thirty. We'll wait till you get to Hardscrabble, I think. You're doing fine."

I tried to read my parents' expressions but saw only confidence. I wished I felt as sure. For the first time, I faced up to the possibility of failure and knew that I did not want to fail. Maybe I'd never get there, I thought to myself, as I took my bearings again and settled into a steady sidestroke once more. I had lost that wonderful surge, but now with the chocolate it was coming back, and with it my courage.

Doing your best, my parents called it. "You're a Thoroughbred," my daddy once told me, and I remembered now — not quite sure what he meant. I swam. And swam. A Thoroughbred. I supposed racehorses got tired, too. Here I was, a tiny speck in this wide bay with only my head showing, eyes pulled large by my bathing cap and water splashing over my face and even in and out of my mouth as my right arm flashed steadily up and down.

When my shoulders began to feel tired, I flipped over and used the backstroke with a frog kick or a slow, loose flutter — then sculled for a bit, moving only my hands, eyes closed. It's funny how effortlessly that ate up the distance. Then, refreshed, as I turned back to the sidestroke, I noticed my folks waving, calling, pointing.

Finally I saw that I had come even with Hardscrabble Point, which, opposite the bulge of Phelps Island, roughly defined the largest area of the Upper Lake. I waved back and swam to the boat for more candy.

With that and a little drink of water in me, I lined up Chapman's pavilion in my sights and swam: ready, stroke, power glide, coast — ready, stroke. Now just the smaller bay to conquer. Thank goodness the bigger one came first. My body had begun turning as if for the backstroke as I coasted. I floated well but no longer carved the water. I was rubbery, my arms tiring.

I thought ahead to Chapman's. After a walk uptown to the stores in the tiny town of Mound, cement sidewalks hot on our bare feet, we sometimes returned to an ice cream cone or soda on the side porch over the water at Chapman's.

All at once I giggled. At nearby Pearson's boat works, Dad once lost his masterful image. We had stopped there because we needed gas. Dad had grasped the empty five-gallon gasoline can, flipped a rope around the dock post, and put one foot on the dock. As he heaved his body up, the boat slipped farther away, and he sank into the water between the dock and the boat. Still clutching the empty gas can, he presently came to the surface, his pompadour perfectly parted in the middle and plastered tight to his scalp, giving him an oddly meek look.

My muscles ached. The lake pushed against me and held me back. I felt I must rest, and I flipped over again. I laid my arms back over my head in the water and let my feet float up to the surface. We were passing Priest's Bay now, and the entrance to Halstead's Bay, where we had once picked water hyacinths. It reminded me of the day we had picked water lilies and the boat got stuck.

The White Bridge! I hadn't even remembered it. Now I was long past that, past Hardscrabble, past Priest's Bay. I must make my limp muscles carry me this last stretch to Mound. I didn't want my parents to know how tired I was. Lining myself up with the rowboat again, I looked ahead to several moored boats and two in the bay on the way there. One man in a rowboat was still fishing, even though it was almost noon. The sun beat down, making the water drops iridescent.

Suddenly I froze. My ankle—what was the matter? My left ankle. Every time I kicked, a sharp pain grabbed deep in my ankle. I was so close now. I couldn't believe I wouldn't reach shore. I was frightened and suddenly on the verge of tears. Starting toward the boat, I saw my parents bending over Everett. No, don't give up—I can do it, I told myself sternly. Keep the ankle straight. Plow on. The water was heavy, slowing my progress. I pushed as hard as I dared but felt no surge of power. My parents were closer now. I kept my face away so they would not see the hurt. People were watching from Chapman's long dock. Tempted to stop there, I made myself swim to shore, as the rules said, until the slimy, muddy bottom hit my good foot. I slipped a little. Dad beached the boat beside me and helped me in.

"Good job! Miggles, are you all right?"

I confessed and was quickly enthroned in the back seat next to Mother. She had draped a big Turkish towel over her long skirt, and as I snuggled happily against her, she wrapped it around me.

"That was a great swim," she whispered. "I'm proud of you."

Her arm was warm around my shoulder. "Now about that ankle." Under the magic of her fingers, the cramp began to ebb.

"Hey, Marj, look at this!" Everett scrambled over the seats to show me the new sail he and Dad had rigged on his little boat. Dad restrained him, saying, "Ev, you'll have to wait till we get home. Your sister has swum well over two miles. That's a long way, isn't it?" Dad grinned and his eyes shone under the brim of his big straw hat. I was dimly aware that he wore wash pants over his swimsuit and a long-sleeved shirt to protect his fair skin from the sun.

"I'm hungry," I said, but when Mother gave me a sandwich I managed only one sleepy bite. I was riding high, my every want indulged. I thought of Bob. Now I would have the last word with him. I was glad I had finished what I set out to do.

The only other thing I remember from the long trip back is Dad's vigorous pulling on the oars, with a strong little snap at the end of each stroke. Each time, as he returned the oars to position for the next pull, he turned them over and feathered them in the way he knew I loved, for it bounced the spray from the little waves, and sometimes rainbow colors sparkled in the sunlight. I knew that my parents were pleased with me, and it felt good. Warm in the noon sunshine and the approval of my parents, I dozed.

Unsinkable Crane Island

OVER THE SEVERAL YEARS of Bob's friendship with his musical school chum Ralph Thompson, Bob practiced playing accompaniments on the banjo he had acquired in grade school. Occasionally Ralph asked Bob to play with his small jazz group, the Bearcat Serenaders. We often invited Ralph's widowed mother to join us at the island, progressing from polite invitations to eager attempts at persuasion.

As our efforts increased, her invariable response grew more stubborn: "An island, it's so dangerous." Her short chunky figure shuddered. She hugged the nearest child in her warmhearted way.

"The island might sink!" she advised us. "I've heard of islands that just sank right down under the water!"

As she talked I could hear Edgar Allan Poe's whirlpool, pictured in one of my books, sucking boat and passengers alike into subterranean horrors.

Some of our guests at Crane Island had traveled widely. They gazed out at the water framed by the kinnikinnick bushes and two magnificent arching elms and agreed it was the most enchanting view they had ever enjoyed. But no matter what we described to Mrs. Thompson, she shook her head. We waxed enthusiastic as we pictured moonlight on gilt-tipped waves, but she only closed her eyes and frowned. Our project seemed hopeless.

Then one day, as she sat in our town kitchen nibbling a piece of Mom's nut-laden bread, the spring sunshine glinting in her dark braids, she ventured, "I try to imagine a boat — the water all sparkly — and out of nowhere a sudden wind comes — and there I am — in trouble!"

We were speechless with surprise. So she had been listening! She was tempted!

"I think it's amazing that in all those years you've never had an accident," she went on. "I suppose — maybe — if I followed all the safety rules — there just isn't any danger."

We all began to talk at once. Before she left, we had agreed at last on a date for her to visit the cottage early in the coming summer. My father was to pick her up after his Friday classes in a friend's car and drive the twenty-five miles to the lake, where Bob would meet them with the launch. She insisted that she would have to return to town the next morning.

On the chosen day, the wind and the waves were still, the late afternoon soft and warm. As they chugged the half-mile across to the island, Dad later told us, Mrs. Thompson sat big-eyed and rigid as a statue. When I ran to meet the boat and give her a welcoming hug, she remarked in genuine surprise, "The island . . . it looks so earthy, so kind of . . . well . . . big and solid."

Her cheeks nearly matched her brilliant pink blouse as she puffed up the steep wooden stairway to the top of the bluff. Soon we were all settled at the long porch table, where we feasted happily on fresh bass and buttery garden vegetables. By this time Mrs. Thompson was obviously feeling good about her adventure. When even the eastern sky began to show a faint coral hue, she was enthusiastic about the sunset. My father, as he so often did, courteously offered a ride in the canoe to the west side.

She did not protest when we left the dishes on the table and flocked to the dock. With a flourish, Dad brought around the almost untippable eighteen-foot Old Town canoe, and we placed the cork cushions as seats in the bottom. Bob, who had changed to his swimsuit, stood in the water and steadied the boat. Our guest awkwardly took her place beside Mother, her stout body at first too tense to relax against the backrest. We children, also on flotation cushions, cuddled against the facing lazyback as Dad eased us gently out onto the placid lake. Our chatter subsided.

To dispel Mrs. Thompson's nervousness, Dad demonstrated the effortless Indian way of propelling the craft without taking the paddle from the water. She wondered at our virtually silent progress as we glided past the red and white buoy that marked Our Point. Then we entered into the riot of color. The wide western sky was slowly changing from vivid rose and scarlet to amber; the serene lake mirrored its brilliance. Mrs. Thompson was entranced, her brown eyes open wide, her hands still in her lap, her body tense.

Then Dad guided us among tall reeds at the north end of the island. Their sudden rustling on the sides of the canoe startled Mrs. Thompson. The green tasseled tops closed over us, though we could still see the fading sky directly above. The swishing rushes hid us in their green clasp until we burst out into the echoing silence on the other side.

"Like Moses in the bulrushes," our guest whispered.

"I'm glad I'm not alone like he was," I said, and her warm hand cautiously reached out to pat mine.

Soon we had circled the little island. Dad, sensing our reluctance to stop, let the boat drift near our dock. It was so tranquil, and Mrs. Thompson now sat back and gazed up at the deep blue sky.

"I'm going to swim a bit to cool off," Bob announced.

He often dived without upsetting the canoe, but tonight we couldn't risk it so he began to roll out over the gunwale. The rest of us leaned in the opposite direction. Carefully he slid off and almost soundlessly entered the water. Suddenly there was nothing to counter our weight. The canoe whipped back and overturned. All of us spilled into the chilly water.

As I struggled to the surface, I found Mother and Dad treading water and holding Mrs. Thompson's head high. So hastily had they reacted that, although she was gasping, her heavy black hair was not even wet on top. Her startled eyes were as wide and round as the circle of her open mouth. Her silky pink blouse, brighter than ever from her ducking, was plastered to her ample bosom.

A few strokes brought us to where we could wade to shore. Mrs. Thompson was shivering, and Mother put her arm around her as we hurried her to the cottage. Mother sent me ahead for big bath towels, and soon we had her wrapped up and tucked into her bed. She loosened her hair, and I was allowed to unbraid it and press it dry.

As we bade her good night, she impulsively held out her arms to me, and I soon found myself tucked in beside her, a small warm presence to offset her chill and fright. She began to relax but still shivered from time to time. I began to sense the terror water held for her. She had placed enormous trust in us.

Wide awake in her fleshy embrace, I thought uncomfortably that Dad had done everything he could — we all had. But the canoe had tipped over. This time Mrs. Thompson was right. All our promises, our assurances, came back to me. We had been so certain — so eager to share our pleasures.

Mrs. Thompson stirred, tightened her arm around me, and exhausted, finally slept.

And, soon, so did I.

Next morning a crestfallen family labored to distract her. Dad seated her in a cheerful shaft of sunshine to enjoy Mother's lavish breakfast soufflé. Strawberries sweetened with brown sugar glowed red in their glass bowls, and gray mugs held fragrant, steaming coffee. Resounding silences that grew ever more uncomfortable punctuated bursts of conversation. Would Mrs. Thompson still be terrified to ride in the launch? Or would that now seem tame to her?

She was trying, too. Although her eyes looked dark and heavy from a restless night, she sensed our distress and tried to be appreciative of the festive breakfast and the bright morning.

Smiling, Dad attempted to joke. "We'll not use the canoe this morning unless you really prefer it. The launch is ready and waiting whenever you feel you must leave."

"You've given me an experience I'll never forget," she teased, and we realized she'd forgiven us.

Dad helped many of our guests on the island with diving, surfboarding, and sailing. He simply loved to teach. He taught many island children to swim and dive — even Helen Jane McKendry, whose terror on the diving board finally gave way to his patient encouragement.

We all loved the surfboard—just a flat board pulled by the launch.

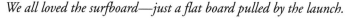

One summer he was inspired by the fact that Minnesota is the land of ten thousand lakes. Everyone who lives here, he felt, should not only know how to swim but also be prepared to help in case of a water disaster. When the floor of the canoe needed cleaning, he overturned the boat so that we could discover the pocket of air trapped inside, knowledge that could save a life some stormy day.

He took a Red Cross lifesaving course, then organized classes for seven swimmers: Bruce Mudgett, Camilla Edholm, Dorothy Harris, Helen Dickson, Mother, Bob, and me, although I would not be twelve and thus eligible for junior status until fall. Day after day we practiced "breaks" and "carries." We learned how to help a swimmer who was tired but could cooperate by floating. We laid an arm across his chest and swam sidestroke with the body over our hip. Or we swam backstroke, pulling the swimmer on his back, grasping his head with our hands. We could change to breaststroke, pushing the swimmer, whose hands rested on our shoulders. As we became more confident, we learned how to break the hold of a frightened drowning person, who typically tries to climb up on the rescuer and so can sink both. These "breaks" became vigorous, even threatening, as we practiced, and the victims thrashed and splashed. We studied how to approach from the back, even if we had to dive under to surprise the drowning person, in order to get a grasp for the "chest carry" before the victim could grab us.

We learned to make porpoise dives to the muddy bottom of the lake to reclaim a swimmer who might have given up the struggle. We talked Mother into providing one after another of our big white mismatched platters for practice targets. At first they gleamed against the bank of chocolaty mush of the drop-off as they rocked downward, but after several "rescuers" had pawed at the loose shifting silt of the slope, the water became clouded. We discovered the grim problems of underwater retrieval, and Mother learned to manage with big plates instead of platters. All summer we practiced our skills.

When Dad finally arranged for an instructor from Minneapolis to come to the island to put us through a stiff examination, written and practical, we all were approved. Year after year we wore our American Red Cross Life-Saving Corps badges sewed to one swimming suit after another, until they were in shreds. My own swimming became more confident. "She swims like a fish" became "She

Crane Island lifesavers, 1923, demonstrating the stranglehold, land carry, pulling a person out of the water, and wrist hold

earned her junior lifesaving badge with the grown-ups!" My self-confidence grew.

As the fiasco of Mrs. Thompson's visit dimmed, we began again to think Dad was infallible. Then Myrtle, Mother's unmarried sister, came to visit. An elementary-school teacher in Evanston, Illinois, Aunt Myrtle knew many ways to a child's heart. Everett forgave her for calling him "Auntie Myrtle's little manikin," and we all loved her. She played the organ in a big church on Sundays, and she soon had Bob's banjo tuned to the piano; they produced duets and sometimes let me twiddle along with them on my mandolin.

But talented though she was, Aunt Myrtle could not swim. Her years of lugging babies on her hip as the eldest child of seven had made her back a little crooked, and she did not excel at anything athletic, but she longed to learn to swim. Like Bob, she had a slender frame and could not float — even face down with her lungs inflated. Dad supported her while she paddled faithfully, but when he withdrew his arm, she routinely sank — slowly, soberly, hopelessly. When she returned years later, she wanted to try again. But she had gained no weight, and even Dad could not help her. Aunt Myrtle would never be a swimmer.

Ev, the Family Rascal

THREE IS A RESTLESS NUMBER, and the roles and pairings in our family changed often. Ev and I teased Bob that he was the favorite child because he was our parents' firstborn and always in charge. Bob and I belittled Everett as the spoiled baby of the family. The boys accused me of garnering unmerited special attention because I was the only girl.

Spoiled or not, Everett was independent from an early age on. Even though he was the youngest, he would never allow himself to be left out. When he was three and too small to row sitting down, he found he could manage by stepping back and forth across the seat to push the oars. He soon followed Bob around. He learned how to make boats from bits of wood and tried to make them float level in the water.

My earliest memory of Everett is his asserting his rights at our house in town. My parents were patiently trying to get a snapshot of Bob and me standing on the stilts Dad

Ev was too small to row sitting down.

had made for us. We climbed up, balanced, and began to tire while we waited and waited for Ev. He was dragging a long pair of skis into the picture. We wobbled and yelled to him to hurry. When Dad finally snapped the photo, he ducked his head and made a face! His curly blond hair and rosy cheeks were so cute that he got away with it.

As he grew, Everett imitated Bob in developing an interest in building tree houses. The most elaborate of them was at Our Point. To reach the tree house we had to walk through the poison ivy that filled the hollows and trailed on the low bushes. Since we habitually went barefoot, there was an element of excitement — at times increasing to

In this revealing photo, serious Bob, rascally Ev, and Marjorie the peacemaker show off skis and homemade stilts.

fearless bravado — in this crossing. I, at least, felt we were part of a select group, beings providentially protected from the poison. Only once in all those years did itchy blisters appear on my wrists. We heard a tale of three girls who ate some of the leaves — and wound up in the hospital.

When Ev was ready to begin his highest tree house, Merton McKendry was spending the summer on the island with his grandmother, Mrs. Amy. Redheaded, thin, energetic, and a couple of years younger than Ev, he helped nail boards to the trunk of the tall poplar tree for steps and toiled up them with boards and supplies. His younger sister, Helen Jane, whose red hair and fair complexion I envied, tagged along after the boys. One day she sneaked up the steps to the platform and caught them experimenting with a cigar. They teased her into taking a few puffs, then left her there alone to wait for her dizziness and fright to wear off. Understandably, she never told on them.

Once in a while Ev persuaded Mother to let him eat his lunch in his leafy hideaway. I'm sure he teased to sleep there, but on that point Mother was firm. He sought other cozy cubbyholes and found me busy at the boat shelter, where Dad had built wooden canoe rests and a grapevine made a partial covering. I loved that quiet, secret spot and tried to train the vines to grow in a graceful arch over it. Ev was always an independent boy, busy, restless, inquisitive, attracting followers who shared his exploits.

In town, Everett made bicycle trips all over southeast Minneapolis — often making himself late to meals, which were carefully timed because of Dad's rigid teaching schedule. Bob and I managed to be on time, and we took our obedience for granted. I puzzled about Ev. Couldn't he see that we were supposed to do what our parents asked? Bob and I liked the security of minding the rules. Ev often tested the limits.

Once when children were gathering for my birthday party in the late fall, a neighborhood boy came running to the door. Gasping for breath, he said to Mother, "Ev was riding his bike on — Washington Avenue after — school and got hit by a car — and I don't know, but — I think he's dead!"

Mother arranged for a neighbor to be with the party group while she set out on the streetcar to find her child — alive or dead. The news was only partly true. Ev had dodged on his bicycle between two parked cars out into the forbidden street, and Mr. Burgess, the unlucky driver, had not seen him until Ev was suddenly in front of him. He hit my brother but managed to stop with a tire on Ev's leg; had it gone six inches farther, it would have been on his head. Ev had been taken to Minneapolis General Hospital. By the time Mother found him, she could do little to alleviate his misery in the austere surroundings where adult visitors were discouraged and young ones forbidden.

Ev had an efficient, overworked older nurse who warned him angrily, "If you drop one more toy on the floor, I'll come right in and take it away from you!" Mother told us later, a glint in her eye, that whenever Ev got too bored, he dropped one of his many gifts and chuckled as he watched the nurse angrily come to his bedside, snatch the offending toy, and march self-righteously away.

A few days later he came home with a cast on his leg. He got around surprisingly fast in a sitting position on the floor with his leg stretched out ahead of him — cheerful as always and unaware that he was a hazard to the rest of us. I admired Ev's ability to figure out his own solutions but thought also of that poor old nurse; I hoped her next patient would be easier. Why did I always have to be on both sides of everything?

The next summer at the lake Everett often roamed the island alone, ignoring Bob and me at our quieter pursuits. One hot day he was greatly surprised to see several large fish lazing in the warm shallow water near the Big Dock. Surely these were as large as the pickerel his father had carefully weighed at about ten pounds and proudly reported to Mr. Eustis! Everett stood on the dock and studied the fish. There were three, and they were nearly motionless. If he jumped in they would awaken and dash away. Instead he sat on the dock for a long time and gradually inserted one foot and then the other, until he was standing in the water near them. His eye on the largest one, he waited until it moved nearer the shore and parallel to it. Ev stooped and, all in one motion, scooped the fish out onto the grass, where it flopped languidly.

Ev whipped off his shirt, gathered the fish into it, and dashed home. His face flushed with the effort, he victoriously presented his prize to Dad.

"Ah, you have caught a dogfish, Everett. I'm sure you found it feeding in shallow water?"

"Yes, by the Big Dock. It was sleeping. Now we can eat it."

"Dogfish are lazy bottom feeders — not very good for eating." Dad noticed Ev's crestfallen look and added, "Some people eat them. You were clever to catch him without a hook, Son."

Mother also had noticed Ev's disappointment and agreed to cook the fish. Dad prepared it, but after I watched the flesh twitch in the frying pan I was not eager to try it. Soon, however, I understood from my parents' glances that I must do so for Everett's sake. It tasted like mashed potatoes without any salt and was about that consistency. Ev didn't relish it either and never repeated his conquest.

At this stage of our growing up, Bob and I both thought of Ev as a little kid, uninterested in girls — although at four he had been unabashedly in love with Katherine Perine, calling her his "little wifie" and presenting her with a gold ring she wore until it no longer fit on her finger.

But now at nine, he seemed interested only in trying his parents' patience as he experimented with barrier jumping on his bike and roamed the island.

When Ev followed Bob and me into our small private high school, his probing questions challenged the general science teacher, Mr. Garlough, into assigning readings and outlining a set of experiments individually crafted for him. In English class, though, when he was to prepare a two-minute speech in which he would impersonate someone and involve the class, the results were somewhat different. He moved in stately fashion to the podium and said, "This is a church, you are the congregation, and I am the minister." He folded his hands and, bowing his head, intoned, "We will now have two minutes of silent prayer."

A short time later, in the principal's office, he was asked, "Well, Ev, what is it today?"

Barely controlling a smile at Ev's confession, Mr. Boardman said, "If I were you, I wouldn't go back to that class today. Try the library."

That evening, when our parents reproved Ev for his prank, he maintained that he had literally done exactly what the teacher asked.

"Besides," he finished with a grin, "I have a lot more fun than Bob and Marj with their high grades and dumb awards."

The highlight of our summers often was the Fourth of July. We saved the sparklers till evening so that we could wave them and make secret writing on the sky. Roman candles with their spray of sparks rocketed a sudden fireball twenty feet into the darkness; they had to be carefully pointed away from oneself and others. We also had noisy firecrackers, all unrestricted in those days. The boys disdained my ladyfingers, tiny things they said popped about as loud as a soda cracker breaking. Once they infuriated me by grabbing an intertwined bunch of them and setting them all off at once. They experimented with long fuses to ignite firecrackers under tin cans and rivaled each other to see how high one could be sent.

One sunset after the daily flag lowering, the Myers kids trooped to the end of the dock while Dad unpacked the Fourth of July balloon, a four- or five-foot creation of paper with ribs of perilously thin slivers of wood. At the mouth of the balloon was a rigid collar protecting a basket of excelsior — thin wood shavings — that had been soaked in paraffin. When it was almost dark, Dad assigned each of us a station around the sagging balloon to hold it steady. He inserted a slip of paper with our name and address into the balloon near the basket. All eyes were on him as he struck a match and ignited the encapsulated bonfire. At first, nothing happened, although we could see the fire glowing through the delicate paper. Slowly the heat built up and the warm air filled the tissue globe, which began to stir restively. It seemed alive: a big moth exercising its wings. The little fire burned low and steady. Dad hovered over us happily as we held on until the air in the balloon was completely expanded.

One by one we were instructed to release our hold. Slowly, mysteriously, soundlessly the brightly glowing balloon, like an overgrown Japanese lantern, rose over the water. A barely perceptible current of air tipped it dangerously. We gasped, fearing it would burn and fall ignominiously into the water. Ev reached out to rescue it and nearly fell in himself. The whole balloon glowed, rose slowly, soared erratically, and finally moved off safely over the lake. It sailed past the treetops and became a diminishing glow in the deepening darkness. If I could fly away with it, what would I see in the world below? Other families gathering with balloons? Would someone find our balloon — someone standing on a dock somewhere who also liked to watch the sunsets, someone who watched the moonlight glitter on the waters of Lake Minnetonka, someone who loved the lake as much as I did, someone — exciting, different, special?

A postcard arrived later, telling us that our fragile ambassador had finally cooled and collapsed into a tree. There was no name, no address. I felt vaguely disappointed. What had I expected? Was there someone out there I needed to meet? Dad, too, seemed disappointed. Sometimes in his enthusiasm he seemed like a boy, while Mother, watching from the porch, was the parent, glad when the festivities were over and everyone was unharmed.

Everett enjoyed the balloon launching, but he always had some project of his own under way. When he was twelve or thirteen he built a small craft — about four feet by ten feet — in our basement in Minneapolis. Its flat bottom, made of Masonite, curved up at the front to a four- or five-inch cowl surrounding the cockpit. Having saved his allowance and Christmas money from Aunt Myrtle, he visited a junkyard on Washington Avenue and bought an old Chevrolet engine, which he brought home on a coaster wagon.

The next summer, by dint of patient tinkering, Ev managed to get the engine to work and experimented with installing it in the homemade boat. Toward the end of the season, when he was finally ready for a grand trial, he seated Bob in the front and, sitting in the back, started the engine. The boat moved forward slowly, but when Ev opened the throttle, Bob's weight caused it to plow under instead of skimming the surface. In spite of the rounded front, a bow wave developed and flowed over the cowl. Three feet from the end of our dock, the boat submerged and sank. The boys recovered the engine, and Ev continued to work on the boat. At the end of the summer, he hid the engine in the bushes of Our Point, but during the winter someone stole it.

With his usual stubbornness, Ev kept at his project. He mounted a small outboard motor that Bob had made in his freshman year of engineering school in place of the stolen one. Ev now called the rejuvenated boat the "berry crate" after the paper-thin wooden crates in which we bought berries. Unburdened with the extra weight of a passenger, Ev had many a merry ride in it.

An unimaginative professor who watched from our front porch remarked, "So this is Ev's wonderful, high-powered boat."

"What an insult," Ev mourned, "after losing my motor to a thief."

Several years later, Everett, still in search of the perfect motor, went back to the junkyard and bought a Starr —

a car manufactured in Minneapolis about 1910 — and drove it across the frozen lake to the island. The weather was cold, but the day was invigorating, sunny, with barely a breeze. Everett's friend Florence, whom we called Flippy, accompanied him. Bob and I led the way in Dad's car. The ice was thick; Dad had not approved the trip until he was sure of that. But Bob insisted on driving ahead to guide us away from places where springs might have weakened the ice.

When we rounded Gallagher's Point we were amazed to see a fish house. The fisherman must have been equally surprised to hear our cars, for he came out to investigate. I had never been in a fish house and was delighted when he let us crowd into his. We checked the ice, which appeared to be about a foot and a half thick. The tiny building was windowless and dark except for light that filtered through the ice and illuminated the water underneath. He demonstrated the motion he used to keep the baited hook bobbing far below.

I paid small attention to him, I'm afraid. I was utterly absorbed in being able to see clear to the bottom of the lake. It was as if I had been taken underwater with my vision unimpaired. How many times had I tried to pierce the surface with my eyes or to imagine what the fish saw? Far below, feathery light-green weeds swayed gently, and a tall, sturdy dark-green pickerel weed reached to the bottom edge of the ice. Suddenly, a foot below the square aperture, a fish appeared with no sound, no splash, nothing to alert us to its sudden appearance. It was a small pickerel. It eyed the hook, then with a sinuous twist of its body disappeared.

I asked the fisherman whether our presence had frightened the fish, but he assured us that this often happened. We watched for a long time in tense silence, squeezed into that little house, but the wanderer never returned, and my yearning did not bring him back.

Finally we came out into the glorious sunshine and traipsed back to the cars, which the boys had carefully parked some distance from each other and from the hole. We shared a jubilant feeling. The ice was relatively clear of snow, and Bob and Everett began to practice braking the cars into a spin, then steering them out of it. Flippy was eager to learn to drive. Everett put her behind the wheel and taught her some protective maneuvers; she caught on at once and was soon doing as well as he did.

When we tired of that, Ev drove the Starr up on shore near the launch; we four had helped Dad winch the launch up out of the water on a track with a pulley hooked around a tree. We opened the cottage and ate our sandwiches in front of the little potbellied stove, which, although it quickly became red hot, could not persuade us to shed all our wraps.

When summer came, Ev sank the chassis of the Starr, saving the fine engine. Dad had finally decided to abandon the big old "one-lunger" launch he had patiently reconditioned and let it decay. He made an offer on a boat that had been stored for seven years at Wise boat works in Wayzata and got it for thirty-five dollars in delinquent storage charges. With Ev's Starr motor installed, it became a four-cylinder boat with a self-starter and took care of our needs in style while Ev went on to experiment with building a motorcycle sidecar that allowed its occupant a good night's sleep while in transit.

Superdad

"ALLOW ME TO INTRODUCE a real honest-to-goodness Englishman — our new caretaker, Oscar Lodge!" The muscular young man was of medium height, his demeanor deferential and formal. His English accent fascinated me. He bowed, and we children looked wide-eyed as we all sat down to supper on our front porch back in 1921, when Dad first became island superintendent.

Dad's duties as an unpaid official were various, but his first priority each spring was to find a strong fellow capable of doing chores for many people at a salary of forty dollars a month and willing to live in the one-room cabin in the center of this tiny, quiet island.

Oscar was a student of Dad's at the university. My father's genius as a mentor always amazed me. People responded to his enthusiasm and found in themselves abilities they didn't know they had. Oscar presumably had been gently reared as the nephew of Sir Oliver Lodge of University College in Liverpool, knighted in 1902 for his work in physical and psychical research. How Oscar came to be in this country I do not know, but perhaps he had not fit the role ordained for him and had been sent to America as a remittance man — that is, partially supported by income from his family in England. He was as gentle and sweet as his famed uncle reputedly was. When I learned that he had some training as a tumbler, I gazed at his stocky build and tried to picture daring deeds.

Then one day friends on the west side of the island planned a dance on their big porch and wanted to borrow our upright piano. A group of men managed to manipulate the unwieldy thing across our front porch and down the steps. There they set up planks to provide a runway for the piano's small casters. When the men, Oscar among them, pushed the piano off one board, it was carried to the front and the piano was rolled onto it. Two men were needed on the downhill side to prevent the piano from overturning. They dared not stop until they reached level ground. There they sat down to rest — except for Oscar.

In a respectful, well-modulated voice he suddenly sang out, "Your attention, please!" He stepped off a measured distance from the piano, turned, dashed toward it from an angle, gave a prodigious leap, and, placing a hand on top of the piano, sprang clear over it, his body stiffly extended. He landed on his shoulder on the ground, rolled to his feet, and bowed, smiling broadly. At first we were too surprised even to clap. His proud smile faded and he looked uncertain, crestfallen, until we broke into enthusiastic cries of appreciation and his good spirits returned — but I never saw him display his talents again.

An unexpected good came from that short rest. Oscar, who apparently had some experience with pianos, remarked that it would be easier to tip the piano on its side, have every man grab hold, and simply carry the awkward thing to the other cottage. And so it was quickly accomplished.

In ordinary skills, however, Oscar was laughably ignorant. He obviously had no experience with menial chores. When he finished cutting the grass with a push lawn mower under Dad's tutelage, he was given a rake. Always willing, he turned and started cheerfully across the vast Commons, pulling the rake behind him. Dad had to explain the purpose of the raking and demonstrated how to gather the grass clippings into piles. Gradually Oscar mastered his duties — even delivering the ice in the wheelbarrow. He learned to place the shrunken blocks from the island ice chests in buckets to melt for drinking water, then to chip and shape a new piece to fit the space and lower it carefully with the black iron tongs into the top-loading ice chests.

And then one day he presented himself at our kitchen door.

"Doctor Myers, I regret to inform you that the barrow has ceased to function." His voice carried a burden of sadness.

The wheel had locked sideways when a screw had fallen out, and Oscar had no idea what to do. His remark became a joking refrain in our family. When any minor catastrophe struck, we announced, "The barrow has ceased to function."

Back in 1908, when there were only a few houses—Woodward, Hermann, Tyler, and Backus—on the island, a part-time caretaker's duties were outlined in the minutes of the annual meeting. He was to deliver ice, collect mail at the post office in Excelsior, cut the grass on the Commons, take in the association's dock in the fall, and provide general maintenance. He could charge fifteen cents to haul a trunk, ten cents to ferry a passenger to shore, and twenty-two cents an hour if he hired out privately. He was provided a rowboat, five pairs of oars, a lawn mower, a cultivator, an extension ladder, a grindstone, a peavey, two scythes, and a wheelbarrow. And he had the use of the tiny cabin next to the icehouse.

Cottages were added rapidly until 1918, when we bought: Amy, which eventually served three generations; Hamilton, which was marooned in a sea of white daisies (with its mullioned windows it always made me think of Hansel and Gretel's forest cottage); then Innes, an implement dealer in Davenport, Iowa; and Dickson and Bradley, whose cottage was later owned by the Edholms of New York City. Finally, fourteen cottages fringed this idyllic island. Ownership was stable, although cottages began to be rented out occasionally. The next year the first full-time caretaker was hired.

Being superintendent meant that Dad was in charge of all the practical details of running the island as well as solving any problem that might come up. He was asked to be Crane Island superintendent year after year, probably because he obviously cared about its upkeep and about safety for us children. And he had ideas for improvements, such

Crane Island had fewer cottages when we spent summers there than it has in this aerial photo from the 1960s. Our cottage (second on the right) overlooked a grassy bluff to the south, where another cottage was later built.

as clearing the swimming beaches and the path to the Big Dock. One year he arranged to sell the hay crop to a mainland farmer; he shopped carefully to get supplies at the best price. He knew how to do the work (or experimented to find out), so he could see that it was done properly. One summer I was conscripted with my brothers to replace the tape markers on the tennis court, and I often helped push the roller to restore the smooth flatness of the clay surface after a rain or after birds had enjoyed dust baths there. Dad was not paid for his services, but usually his efforts were rewarded with gratitude. I never heard him complain about the work, but even a slight, implied criticism—a chance remark about the grass on the Commons being longer than usual, for example — hurt his feelings. One year he arranged for a well to be sunk for drinking water for everyone, then brought Department of Health representatives to test it. Another time inchworms infested the island, and he provided supplies for banding the trees and smearing them with sticky Tanglefoot to control the pest. He hunted up a new boat when the association's old one gave out.

One rainy spring Dad advertised for a caretaker, hired a young man, drove him to Zumbra Heights, rowed across to the island, and explained the duties and salary. The fellow accepted, shook hands on the deal, then took another job without warning or explanation. Dad, though he was busy at the university, hastily repeated the process and hired Mr. Masker, whom he moved to the island on April 18 during a downpour, then returned to Minneapolis; we usually moved to the island in May. It rained for a whole week. How lonely the island must have been for young Mr. Masker. He tended to his chores on spring weekends when we visited, but the record states that during the week he loafed or rowed to the mainland and hitchhiked to a nearby town, covering his absence with equivocation and excuses. One of his duties was to deliver milk from Woodend farm. He sold tickets for future milk delivery to two faculty wives and ran up milk and grocery bills for himself before he quit. Dad consulted an attorney, who advised that the $8.50 in salary still owed to him be divided between the two women he had cheated and that the remaining problems be left for settlement between the young man and the merchants.

Although our dollar investment in our island hideaway was small, Dad's personal investment of time and energy — scything the nettle patches, for instance — consumed much of what he had left after teaching. One summer he made three trips to Mound to hire a man to help the caretaker with this arduous task, and each time the man failed to show up. (How those cunning little field mice — undisturbed since the big birds deserted the island after the tornado in 1906 — must have scampered about when the scythes first bit into the tall grass near the Commons!) Mr. Eustis consented to finish the grueling scything that time on the understanding that he would never be asked again. Dad was often a pinchhitter on the scything, in addition to keeping the picnic area mowed, tending the swimming barge and diving tower, and building good relations with our neighbors on the mainland.

Many years Dad consulted with the street railway company about increasing service to and from the island. By 1919 the handsome yellow boats steamed up to Crane Island's Big Dock eight times a day, which must have made Dad think he need worry no more about ferry service.

Dad performed these services without complaint because Crane Island had become such an important part of our lives. About this time, he refused a career move to Austin, Texas, feeling that here we children were surrounded with friends and doing well in our schools, and we all loved Crane Island. A larger salary would not be worth giving up all that.

Soon Americans fell in love with the automobile, and people began to abandon the streetcars — and the streetcar boats. They would drive to the lake and pick up the boats they had left on the mainland. By the end of the decade most of the islanders had cars, and by 1924 only two Yellow Canaries stopped at the island each day.

We still had no car. Some years when Dad taught summer school he took the 6:16 boat in the morning to connect with the streetcar at Wildhurst on the Upper Lake, changed in downtown Minneapolis at Sixth and Hennepin, near Witt's Market House, to an Oak-Harriet or Como-Harriet streetcar that ran near the campus.

Dad was fond of fresh peaches, and on his return trip one day, he yielded to temptation and purchased a crate in their luscious prime. The box was of splintery wood; he had to juggle it on his lap, for the streetcar was crowded. He carried the box to the boat landing and onto the boat, and finally lugged it the length of the island to our kitchen. We gloried in fresh peaches, and Mother planned to make the pickled peaches so famous at her faculty dinner parties. But the fruit all disappeared in a frenzy of feasting — some in peach ice cream. A second crate must be hauled home.

A woman who seldom left the island from the time she came in the spring till she departed in the fall noticed Dad's burden and gushed, "Oh, what beautiful peaches! Professor Myers, won't you please bring me a crate, too?"

Unable to refuse a fellow peach lover, Dad obliged, but somehow managed to make it clear that even he had his limits.

By 1927 streetcar boat service was discontinued entirely. The beautiful Yellow Fleet, which in its heyday had kept an hourly schedule with style and clocklike regularity from middle May through September, became useless.

The boats that had sailed Lake Minnetonka were sunk to the bottom. Now the Myerses too invested in a car.

We islanders were independent with our own boats and cars, but we still had no arrangments for parking on the mainland. Dad spent many anxious hours exploring the possibilities and pleading our cause with neighbors on the shore. He dealt with many time-consuming questions — should the caretaker have to deliver ice on Sunday? Should a shelter be built at the Big Dock for waiting passengers? But none loomed as large as this one: Where could people park when they drove to Zumbra Heights and came across to Crane in small boats? My father liked to see everyone's needs taken care of and people at peace with one another. Balancing the limitations of the slender treasury with his own high standards, he struggled to answer these questions.

The early problems of the island appear to be trivial and even amusing compared with our being marooned, but the record of the yearly association meetings shows built-up feelings divided the members into self-righteous, contentious groups that made the meetings hard for the president to control. The mandates from these meetings were occasionally difficult for the superintendent to put into practice. Notice was given that Crane Island was in a game preserve, and thus Dad no longer felt free to teach Bob to shoot rabbits in early spring to protect the gardens. Hard times were reflected in the association's vote not to extend caretaker service to any family that did not pay its dues, originally five dollars per cottage, later ten dollars.

Surely a public servant struggling with skittish caretakers and property owners with no way to get to their prop-

*Until the island was declared a game
preserve, Bob shot rabbits in the spring.*

erty did not need to be bothered with the following: The
owner of the best year-round house on the island left on a
two-week vacation. When she returned, she found food
spoiled in the icebox; the caretaker had not brought ice in
her absence.

"Outrageous," she declared. "I pay my dues like everyone else."

What would she have said if he had entered her house in her absence?

She submitted a bill for six dollars to the association, which discussed the matter thoroughly and returned the bill to her for itemization. In the end it was approved and the six dollars duly paid.

My parents laughed when they read in the minutes that "tennis is a quiet game," and thus apparently finally could be played on the Sabbath. It must have been about this time that swimming on Sundays also was approved, for a note follows that it had been accepted by even the more religious members of the association. One can only suppose that this step was not taken without some strife, for it is recorded that Emerson Woodward, son of the founder, had "sided with the 'modern ones'"—the pro-Sunday-tennis faction—and thus tipped the scale in their favor.

Mrs. Edholm sensibly suggested that property owners give their proxies to vote on these questions to their renters, who were more in touch with island culture, but the owners wouldn't hear of it.

The association recorded a warning to Mrs. Innes that she must not increase the number of boys she had invited to camp on the island because it would constitute a commercial enterprise in violation of her deed.

Life was never simple for the superintendent, and the strain began to show on Dad. Now the problem of parking on the mainland was paramount. He had even less time to play and relax. When I asked him to come to swim or for help with my tennis, he answered abruptly, "Not now, Marjorie." I might see a frown instead of the teasing or the smile I expected.

While Dad was thus occupied, Mr. Mudgett, his most aggressive tennis partner, coached some of us younger players. Ev learned tennis with the rest of us but did not enter the tournaments, as Bob and I did. Once Mr. Mudgett offered to help me with my overhead serve. I was used to playing in the afternoon, when the coffee trees gave the court partial shade, but I was grateful for the opportunity and happily agreed to meet him at 10:30 the next morning. The sun was hot and heat shimmered up from the light-gray clay of the court. Hatless and clad in shorts and shirt, I concentrated on how he held his racket. I practiced reaching for height on one toe the way he did. I scampered to

At the tennis court, people sat and watched or waited for a turn to play a singles or doubles game.

retrieve our trial balls, then paused to listen to his words. As time passed, I began to feel light-headed. The lesson continued, and I tried desperately to keep my attention focused. Afraid it would be impolite and ungrateful to confess my weakness, I eventually became faint. Mr. Mudgett helped me to the bench and then walked me home.

That year I felt a new identity as a kid player with a man's fast, straight serve, and I considered myself very grown-up to have had a private teacher.

During the summer of 1925 Dad's health began to fail. He tired easily and was hungry all the time. For a frightening month and a half the doctors ran tests while Dad continued to lose strength. The doctors put him on a strict diet, and his weight plummeted faster; he spent his days on the porch bed, weak and worried and irritable. It was as if my world had turned upside down. He barely had strength to sit up. I felt anxious but did not realize that his recovery was in doubt.

The doctors finally diagnosed a hyperthyroid condition, difficult to find because the gland was in an unusual position. Dad, who was a planner, a doer, and a worrier, was ordered to stay in bed and forbidden to have any "worries, responsibilities, or concerns." Weak from the ill-advised diet, he was now told to "eat all the time and in-between times, too." Here was a role for me. I carried treats to him and felt a surge of pride if he asked for more.

Mother must have faced the real possibility that Dad might not recover. His absences when he was on the Schilling tours had given her a taste of assuming responsibility for the family's welfare as well as the loneliness she felt while he was gone. Whether she shared her concern with Bob, who was sixteen that summer, I do not know, but I at thirteen and Everett at eleven learned to protect Dad's quiet time for a nap, and we all petitioned for him in our own way in our prayers.

I began to think that my life had been spared — from smallpox and storms — so that I could be here beside Mother to help Dad get well.

Now that Dad was eating instead of starving, he gradually gained enough strength to have the necessary operation. His physical improvement after the operation was rapid, but regulating his medication was difficult, and his tendency to worry and his inability to relax made it even more troublesome.

Mrs. Eustis took over the superintendent's duties. Mr. Eustis and Mr. Dickson helped with the work when caretakers could not be found. Professor Vaile, who rented a cottage for several summers and whose son, David, was my frequent tennis partner, worked to keep himself in shape. Bob and Jack Jackson earned a small salary for routine mowing part of one summer. Bob met the Sames and Thurk grocery truck from St. Bonifacius twice a week and delivered orders to the islanders; he also delivered daily newspapers, which came by boat, for one dollar per hundred. Even Helen Dickson took her boat to Zumbra Heights, toiled over the hill to the highway to get the mail, and delivered it door to door, earning one dollar a day.

Dad was soon active again but agonized over the strict regimen that kept the thyroid in balance. By then he had achieved only a temporary setup for "suffrance" to park on mainland property (how galling this term must have been for him), and it was noted in the association minutes that parking noise (honking? loud talk?) would not be tolerated by the mainland hosts.

Ed Perine, who had invested in a vacant lot on Crane, now helped Dad unite the islanders in finding an answer to their parking needs — asserting their rights to access if it came to that. A temporary solution was found when a lot at Zumbra was made available for one summer for ten dollars. Dad had to leave for another Schilling tour without a firm plan in place for the future.

Ambivalence

DURING THE WINTER OF 1925 several things troubled me — several things besides what I saw as my wretched habit of being on both sides of every question. Yet, I asked myself, it's good to be tolerant, isn't it? Our parents always taught us to listen to both sides of a question, to get the other point of view. It left me always seesawing and unsure. I'd no sooner figure out what I ought to be doing than some greater need arose.

I had once thought that my father was infallible, yet after persuading Mrs. Thompson, with her very real fears, to trust us, he had given her the wrong kind of unforgettable experience. In trying to pattern myself after my parents so that I would always be "right," was I deceiving myself? I still prayed to grow to be patient and sweet like my mother.

Bob gave the impression that he always knew what to do if anything went wrong, but he was the one who inadvertently capsized us, Mrs. Thompson included.

Maybe Everett had the answer after all, and I should not try so hard.

There I was — ambivalent again!

My doubts and concerns overflowed that winter as we all faithfully attended church services and Sunday school, where Dad directed the classes. I struggled with questions of life and death and immortality that were much too big for me.

As summer approached, Mother enrolled me in the weeklong Methodist camp held at Janette Merrill Park on Howard's Point, which jutted out from the mainland. I was apprehensive, but reassured by the fact that I would not be more than ten miles or so from the island. I would have to make my way alone, though. I wished I had the self-confidence of my brothers. Neither Mother nor I knew any of the one hundred or two hundred girls from all over the state who would be at the camp. This was a completely new experience. I attended school with confidence, sure that I could hold my own, but I could not remember ever going anywhere else alone. It was scary and tantalizing, too. At school the teachers expected me to be a math whiz (which I was not) because they remembered Bob and a "brain" because of Dad. Here I would be an unknown, free to be whatever I turned out to be.

Mother and Dad took me by boat, and we sauntered through the lovely grounds. When we realized that it was almost time for the noon meal, they quickly registered me, made sure I knew where to bunk, and left. I had no time to feel the shyness I had dreaded. People were moving toward the dining room, and I was swept along. Each girl had apparently come alone and was eager to make friends. A girl from International Falls who had long yellow braids hanging over her shoulders was excited to discover that I lived in the Cities, and I was impressed at the distance she had come, her father's work in a paper plant, and her nearness to Lake Kabetogama and Canada. We ate lunch together, and I discovered that her name was Mary. Soon everyone at the table was telling where she lived and went to school. At each place was a small "memories" booklet, and we began to exchange them to record names.

Mary and I lost track of each other in the classes and games that afternoon, but during the missionaries' talks we got together again. That night we whispered excitedly as long as we could stay awake, describing all the girls we had met and what was special about them. Mary seemed so grown up because she could change her baby sister's diapers and dress her and sing her to sleep. She knew how to do the washing and even make bread. We had both met and liked Sue from Alexandria, who sang beautifully. We three started out together at breakfast next day but kept getting separated in the games and meeting new bunches of girls.

After our morning swim a couple of days later, there was a poster contest. My heart sank. I knew that I had no talent as an artist. Full of camp stories about injustices to Jews, I made a torn-paper silhouette of the Wandering Jew. His long black beard showed up well against a snowy mountain in the background. It won the contest! That, of course, meant everyone knew who I was, and all the girls wanted to write in my memories booklet and be my pal.

It was a nice feeling. I had taken charge of myself and just done what came to mind to do, without asking anyone.

Another outcome of the contest was that the missionaries took notice of me, especially the charming one who told such touching stories of her work in China. There was great need, I learned, for young women who would devote their lives to the work of the Lord overseas. Perhaps this was why the Lord had saved me from those storms and from smallpox, I mused. When I talked with Mary, I found that she too felt that perhaps her busy useful life was preparation for a life of service overseas. Was this what the missionaries meant when they spoke of hearing a "call"?

The last night I dreamed of hungry little children gathered around me as I gave them food, and they learned to love the Lord and read and lead useful lives. Large and close in the dream the moist, dark eyes of my favorite missionary glowed — sometimes disembodied, but always radiating confidence and sympathy. Sometimes she hovered silently in the background in the graceful, flowing robe she had worn at the sing-along by the water. That was the night she told about the dark-eyed baby girl who had died in her mother's arms because she had gone so long without sufficient food, although her older brothers were fed.

The camp workers and one other missionary told stories, too, of people who had gone to other countries to help people, but China is the one I remember; China is where I imagined going someday to teach the little girls that they were important and could make a difference in the world.

That evening as we sang "In Christ There Is No East or West" I felt my heart swell with sympathy. I had assumed that I would spend my life writing happy, worthwhile books until I met the man of my dreams, but now there was a new possibility — an aching need.

At supper before our last big firelight sing-along, the leader asked us to choose one girl to be the Spirit of Camp Wesleyan. A couple of girls distributed paper ballots and pencils. I looked around the crowded dining room, identifying one after another of the fine girls I had met, girls who told of lives so different from mine. Mary, the eldest child in her family, helped with the younger children, washed dishes, and cleaned while her mother did housework for others. Several farm girls had told of raising calves or working in the garden to help support the family or to raise money for their churches. And there was Sue who sang in the choir — even sang solos — and those other girls whose strong youth groups had "helping projects." I struggled to decide but finally chose Mary.

We sang camp songs while the ballots were being counted. Suddenly the room became quiet as the leader stepped to the front of the room. To my amazement, I heard my own name. Had I not done my ballot right? But no, they were announcing that I was the new Spirit of Camp Wesleyan. I was stunned. Girls were cheering, and the leader called me to come to the front and receive a plaque. I couldn't quite believe what was happening to me but obediently went forward in dazed silence through the noisy group, conscious that everyone's eyes were on me.

I had not known such an honor existed and would not have presumed to be considered. To myself I attributed it to the accident of winning the poster contest.

Now the memories booklets again became the interest of the moment. Everyone, it seemed, wanted to write in mine, and I was busy answering in theirs. I was pleased that the girls I especially admired took time to write. One wrote a little poem:

> When I get old and cross and thin,
> And come to see you — let me in!

Others left assorted messages: "I really liked meeting you. Come see me if you're ever near Mankato." "Your Wandering Jew made me so sad. Are you going to be a missionary? I think I will." "I wish I could swim like you." "I feel like we'll always be friends." (That was Sue.)

One lasting result of my first solo social adventure was the continuing loving contact of a missionary who kept in touch for years. I treasure the Chinese bowls she brought to my wedding years later, each inscribed with characters that meant long life and happiness.

I also became increasingly aware of how easy my life was — how privileged, how safe and protected I was. What would it be like to be born with an infirm body and a stunted intellect in a country crowded with needy people where no one cared? How could it be fair for some people to live and die before they had a chance to know God or see the moonlight rippling across the waves of Lake Minnetonka? What responsibility did all my advantages place on me? Was I even capable of the selfless, other-oriented life that my missionary friend led? And did I need to be a missionary? Indeed, did I want to be?

Leave-takings were difficult, involving tears and promises to meet next year. The next summer I made a brief appearance at camp and did, indeed, see Sue and many others, but had only a note from busy Mary, who had a new little sister to take care of and sometimes had to miss school to do so.

It felt good to be back at the island. I could put off till fall my vague concerns about the world, and the petty, worrisome fuss about shorter skirts and matching outfits and gloves and hats or caps, and learning to play the piano, and how to get to my lessons on the streetcar. Here I could forget everything except the minute I was enjoying right now. It occurred to me that my parents might delight in having their own oasis of freedom in summers on the island. They could think about imitating bird calls, watching the sunsets, or planting trees. Here our professor friends wore tattered sweaters and walked barefoot through the wet grass if it rained.

Perhaps that is how the Lord intended for us to live, enjoying and caring for our companions and our surroundings instead of trying to fix everything in the whole world.

Then I thought of Mary, whose helping at home had prevented her returning to camp and might keep her from becoming a missionary. There was not much glamour in that, yet it had to be done. It all got to be very complicated.

I Find Out about Boys

WHEN I WAS TWELVE, my two brothers were still the principal boys in my life. My school-year activities revolved around my neighbor chum, Ruth Burkhard, a vivacious girl who enjoyed people. We started kindergarten together and were closer than sisters through grade school and high school. We explored along the riverbank to find white sand for "paintings," took music lessons, started various clubs, and alternated in holding the Motley School championship for marathon games of jacks. She and I were looking forward to graduation from grade school at Christmastime in 1923, since we had both skipped partial grades. Our parents planned that we would attend University High School, where one could only enter in the fall, so there was much discussion of how we should fill the interval. Both our fathers taught German at the university, and, as it happened, Professor Burkhard had a class in beginning German scheduled for spring quarter. He had the happy inspiration of letting us attend that class.

But that was still in the future when, in the spring of 1923, I was in the first half of eighth grade and Mother again visited old Motley School to be sure her children's grades were satisfactory before moving us out to the island for the summer. Bob was so eager to go that he crossed off each day on his calendar from Easter on. Once before we had made the move as early as the beginning of May, as requested by the family renting our house. It suited Dad, for the rent helped to piece out his modest salary, and it suited us children, for we could never get too much of the island. On the other hand, transferring to Mound consolidated school for the last few weeks meant dragging ourselves out of bed at daylight and choking down a bowl of cereal in time to cross the lake to meet the school bus.

One morning the lake was still and a light mist was slowly lifting as Bob rowed us around the red-topped buoy at Our Point. I sat carefully in a new blue plaid cotton dress Mother had made for me. A cormorant perched on the buoy's tip, a vantage point for finding his breakfast. The bird watched us, spread its wings, then sulkily, it seemed to me, crouched back. When the oarlocks squeaked, the bird was suddenly airborne, its wings beating an angry path in its precipitate flight. I hated to leave without knowing if it returned to the buoy, but it had disappeared. The sky was empty. I dreamed along until the boat ground to a stop on the sand and jarred me wide awake. The grass was still wet with dew as my brothers and I made our way through the meadow and up the hill to join the Wolff girls and others for the five-mile trip on the school bus.

For me the experience was a rather forlorn couple of weeks in an unfamiliar setting. Returning in late afternoon, we were just in time for dinner and begged to be allowed a quick dip before an early bedtime. The payoff was that country school let out at least two weeks before city schools. The joys of summertime could begin.

The Wolff girls were daughters of a dairy worker at Woodend farm. After school was out, we invited them occasionally to our Sunday school. When it was not raining or too windy, we had our service in a collection of boats grouped together on the lake. We sang "America" and "Jesus Loves Me," the melodies floating softly over the water. If Reverend Harris was at the island, he gave a short sermon and prayer standing in the steadiest of the motorboats, surrounded by rowboats and canoes. Often after the benediction, more hymns would sound as the boats parted and worshipers made their way home to Sunday dinner.

With no telephone, it was difficult to make arrangements with the Wolff girls, and no lasting friendship developed. This year, I missed Ruth and my other city friends. For the first time I felt a little let down by our move to the lake. I had read the books in the cabin; I was restless and complained to my mother. The island had never produced a girl companion — except for occasional visitors. Those who lived on the island were either too old (the Harris twins were nearly five years my senior) or too young.

Worse than that, the island seemed to attract boys. Summer after summer I would see redheaded Donnie Innes (whose curls were cut over his mother's protests when he was five) and his two brothers: Bob, who beat me just often enough at tennis to keep things interesting, and John, crippled by polio, who often accompanied us in a coaster wagon. Donnie Stixrood was also a redhead and also younger than my younger brother. The twin Cummings boys were even younger. Mother counted seven that year and teased me by showing a snapshot of me with a couple of them all tousle-headed and barefoot, leaning against a haystack and chewing straws.

My brown-eyed cousins, who were a little older than I, kept things lively for me one summer when the song "Margie, I'll Tell the World I Love You" was popular. Discovering that I was shy, they sang it to me with great feeling. If there was an audience, they often finished on their knees. About the time I began to enjoy the attention, they had to go home to Illinois.

Mother not only teased me gently about the little boys, she also remembered my remark about being bored. I think she understood my mood and how ready I was for something new. Thus she challenged me to take charge of meals and ordering supplies for two weeks and offered to pay me fifty cents a day if I would take full responsibility. Until I reached high school, my allowance had been ten cents a week, half of which was for Sunday school, some of which must be saved, and all of which I learned to record in a little account book. I accepted Mother's offer eagerly, only to learn that it was more of a task than it seemed. The Sames and Thurk store of St. Bonifacius delivered our grocery orders at the Zumbra landing twice a week, on Monday and Thursday at four o'clock. They brought only what people had ordered on their previous trip, and they took written orders to be delivered on their next trip. Thus I had to plan meals a full week ahead.

Our menu was relatively simple. We supplemented store goods with fresh fish and with string beans, beets, corn, and strawberries from the garden. But at midweek I ran out of dry cereal, for which I substituted cooked oatmeal, and crackers for soup. There was some grumbling from the boys. My worst moment was when I forgot to order flour, apparently expecting staples to be always at hand. I wound up ignominiously unable to serve the pancakes I had promised. Since we had eaten the last loaf of bread as toast for breakfast, I dug new potatoes to serve with sardines for dinner. My version of a Waldorf salad — apples and marshmallows and raisins with lettuce from the garden instead of celery — partially restored my standing.

I was nearly finished with my two-week project when I overheard Dad and Mother talking about a new family who planned to rent the Amy cottage. I knew that Dad was still concerned about getting a caretaker. He had been talking to the older brother in this family about taking the job and had consulted the father, who was a minister, about his son's abilities. I sensed there was something special about that, although I didn't understand just what. But when Dad mentioned that there was a younger sister, a girl just a year older than I, I lost interest in all the rest. Life was finally smiling on me.

The day the Flagler family moved in I hurried to finish my duties, then ran to their cabin to invite them all to swim with us in the afternoon. I raced home again to report that Tess was indeed just a few months older than I and was slender with curly dark hair. Fulfilling my fondest hope, she loved tennis and swimming, knew how to paddle a canoe, and was as eager as I to find a friend. She also seemed to know about boys — to be interested in them, even, which surprised me some.

My parents liked her, too, and within a couple of days trusted us to take the canoe by ourselves along our side of the island close to shore. I was ecstatic. The day of our first outing was very warm, and the inviting expanse of water between us and Eagle Island was as quiet as I had ever seen it. The tiny ripples from our boat as we pushed off from shore spread clear out to the post that anchored the water-trolley wire from the windlass above. We waved to Mother, who watched from the porch, and, as we had promised, stayed close to shore, barely far enough out to miss the ends of the docks.

I steered the canoe to where a weeping willow gracefully drooped its narrow, silver-backed leaves clear to the water. Moving almost without a sound, our light craft drifted forward and entered the circle of branches where they hung over the lake. Stalled, we rested in a silent chamber with walls of green lace. Somewhere in the web of branches above us we heard the intermittent drone of a bee testing the silence. A glittering dragonfly zoomed into sight, touched down on a floating leaf, and was gone again like a half-remembered thought.

Sunlight coming through the leaves mottled the surface of the shallow water. I whispered as I showed Tess the pattern waves had made in the sandy bottom where a minnow now darted.

We played together constantly. One day when I had hurried to wash my breakfast dishes and make my bed so we could get an early start on our secret plans, I found her at her back gate, grimacing in pain, her dusky skin blotched red from crying. Her game knee occasionally gave her trouble, but today the pain was intense. She and her brother had quarreled, and he had pushed her so roughly that she had fallen. I was astonished. My brothers and I did not always see eye to eye, but I couldn't imagine being hurt by them. Once I heard Mother reminding Bob he must not hit us younger ones. (I must have taken advantage of that fact, for later I found my dresser drawer of panties and slips and stockings liberally sprinkled with salt and pepper.) Tess recovered but occasionally told me tales of her disagreements with John.

As I saw more and more of the Girl Almost My Age, I became aware of how husky and good-looking her brother was. I had thought of him as much older than I and consequently in a different world, but as he began the work of caretaker, I often saw him at his chores. Frequently I was eating a late breakfast on the front porch when he brought the ice, and he would hang around asking if I was going to be swimming or at the tennis court. Soon he was asking me to meet him there. Mother seemed to have a lot to do on the porch until after he left. She began to caution me about decorum with boys and to suggest the wisdom of enjoying their company in a group. She had never done this before, even last year when the Jackson boy had been attentive, bringing me gifts of hair bows and gum and games and then waiting to be invited to stay and play.

John was only seventeen. This was the first time Dad had used such a young man as caretaker. At first all was well, but soon complaints began coming in. The return address on Mother's eagerly awaited family letter was so water-spotted that it was almost indecipherable. The island ladies let John know that they had always been able to count on grocery delivery by 4:30; several complained that his tardiness made their dinners late. Even the three-times-a-week ice rounds became hit and miss, and twice he skipped them completely. In spite of Dad's instructions, John became more and more dilatory about mowing, until it was finally agreed he should be excused from that chore entirely and be paid only twenty dollars a month. The money so saved could be used in the spring to burn off leaves and grass.

Meanwhile, Mother forbade tennis games with John unless we played doubles. It made no sense to me, but she did not offer an explanation. I was aware that there was tension among the islanders about John's inadequacies, so I let it go at that.

After lunch one day, we kids were asked to amuse ourselves outside for a while. As I started down the hill to the hammock with *Wuthering Heights* under my arm, I saw John's father coming around our back path. He disappeared into the house and didn't come out until I was thoroughly engrossed in the story. Afterward we were told only that John had had some difficulties and was working this summer to try to reinstate himself in his parents' good graces. We must all be patient with him, we were told. Of course we were curious, but nothing more was said and we knew better than to pry.

Then one day Dad rowed to the parking place at the Zumbra landing to find that our old Essex car was missing. Although the little road was secluded — perhaps because it was so secluded — we had never had any hint of trouble before. Even our boats were apparently never touched, although it's true the oars were neatly chained to the seat struts with a padlock. Dad said afterward that he clearly remembered locking the car, but as he stood looking at the grass crushed in two ruts and saw no clue to any disturbance, he had a moment of self-doubt and disbelief.

Dad hesitated to make inquiries at the big houses on the shore, fearing to disturb our benefactors, but instead returned to the island to ask discreetly if other drivers had seen anything suspicious. Professor Vaile remembered coming home from Mound the night before and being surprised to see a car awkwardly backing down the long hill. For just a moment his headlights had lit up the car's interior. He had seen only one person, but the other headlights had prevented his identifying the car. Dad and Mr. Vaile returned to the mainland and drove to the long hill, where they found the Essex neatly parked at the edge of the highway. Inserting the key and stepping on the starter, Dad was relieved when the engine responded promptly. Not until he attempted to move onto the road did he realize what must have happened. The engine revved, but the car did not move: the gears were stripped. The two men figured that whoever had driven it had been accustomed to a different shifting pattern. As the car lost power on the hill, the driver must have tried to downshift into second gear and instead hit reverse. Dad would have to have the car towed and a new transmission installed.

Remembering that he had seen the association's boat cross the lake the previous evening, Dad returned to the island, confronted John, and obtained a full confession. Feeling that John would never be trusted on the island again, Reverend Flagler decided to move his family back to the Cities, but he was grateful that Dad had not involved the authorities. John agreed to reimburse my father for the repairs, and Dad insisted that John himself earn the money. Apparently he kept his bargain, for twice he came to the house with small payments, and others later came in the mail.

I'm sure the advantages of a good reputation were pointed out to us again, and I began to think more about Mother's concerns. I wondered how she had known he was not dependable.

A Swain Is Tested

DIFFICULT AS IT WAS to lose Tess, I found I also missed the excitement and flattery of her brother's attentions. However, the hard-fought tennis tournaments and diving contests shared by all the boys and girls of the island and the evenings of cards or music on the lake made the years pass quickly. The summer I was fifteen and anticipating my senior year of high school, a recent college graduate came to visit his family. He was suave and attractive, and soon — to my surprise — he was paying court to me. He dazzled me with canoe rides and tennis games, his intense blue eyes gazing at me constantly. Dark, slim, and taller than I, he was graceful as he handed me into and out of the canoe and recaptured the errant tennis balls I was used to retrieving myself.

After a vigorous game one day, we sat on the Commons, and he confided in me about his life and a disappointment in love. He began sophisticated talk of rebuilding his "house of the future." At first I did not realize that he meant to rebuild it with me. He drew an extravagant word picture of me: I was fresh, unspoiled, and beautiful, full of physical energy and intellectual promise. Too inexperienced to understand that he was on the rebound, I had poise enough to assure him that I had firm plans for college. Anything else would have been unthinkable in my family. Still, I was elated when the next morning he sought me out for a walk and again talked persuasively. He asked if I would let him wait for me until I had finished school.

When I returned to the house, Mother was kneading bread. I tried to conceal my excitement with idle chat, but I was too full of myself and my new importance as a sought-after woman to keep quiet.

"How old were you when you had your first proposal?" I ventured with what I thought was great subtlety.

Her bare arms and hands covered with flour, Mother turned to me and asked, "Marjorie, has that new young fellow proposed to you?"

My lovely, grown-up secret was out before I had time to relish it. Mother gently made me understand that my glamorous suitor was not emotionally ready for a new commitment. I had to acknowledge that I'd felt a sense of unreality. His words were sweet, but not convincing. Soon, with my heightened awareness, I became self-conscious. I dressed carefully in a red circle skirt that I thought made me look taller and therefore older. Our last meeting before his departure for Iowa was awkward and artificial. His promised letter came after we had moved back to town, and I was already busy with school. Its tone was loving and intimate, but there was no mention of marriage. I pondered, then sent a short note that expressed my appreciation of a pleasant acquaintance but made no mention of any future meeting. Apparently he understood, or he had realized I was not the person he needed at this time in his life.

Another large part of my growing-up experience was enjoying the Harrises. Usually just the twins, Betty and Dorothy, and their mother, Grace, came to the island.

How can I describe that family? Everything that happened in their presence was transformed into excitement. Mrs. Harris's behavior was wildly different from that of any mother I had ever met and sometimes gave me the heady, tingly feeling I got the night the boys finally talked me into diving from the ten-foot tower into the dark water below.

We had splendid fun with our own parents, too, of course. But even when it was spontaneous, it always had an element of teaching in it; we were being prepared for Life. Our behavior stayed within predictable limits, and we certainly never had the feeling that the bottom had dropped out of things and anything could happen.

One summer when the Harrises were renting the Tyler cottage, several of us young ones were eating watermelon at their big oilcloth-covered table. The seeds collected by our plates, and Ev remarked about their shape — rounded and fat in the center. He compared a couple and lined some up in a row.

The crinkles around Mrs. Harris's eyes deepened. "Just like tiddlywinks," she remarked slyly.

That was all it took to precipitate bedlam. As we experimented, a game developed; we got points for skillfully snapping the slippery things into saucers, cups, glasses. Soon we were screaming with laughter as we picked errant seeds out of our hair and off our clothing. We slipped on seeds that had fallen on the floor. Mrs. Harris later insisted that she had found watermelon seeds in the open globe of the kerosene lamp that hung from the ceiling.

After renting a couple of years from the Tylers, the Harrises rented the Amy cottage. Then in 1928 they bought the comfortable Eustis cottage next door to us. There we often collected on the deep porch that ran around three sides of the house. At the north end hung swinging beds. At the opposite end, near the kitchen, vines crowded the screens and an eating table was nestled. In between, chairs sat about casually as if friends were expected to drop in at any time. From the outside the house radiated welcome. Its small second story squatted like a fat square candle on a birthday cake. The dark interior was seldom used except for the fireplace and the piano.

We had discovered that in the company of Betty and Dorothy, our pals from Pirate Club days, subtle and delightful things often happened. When Bob at a tender age quickly solved a complicated math puzzle, they treated him like an undiscovered genius, and Ev's early mechanical wizardry caused them to bestow on him an embarrassingly bright halo when he was still a wiry, barefoot eight-year-old with unshakable faith in himself. They opened new vistas of philosophy and psychology that I had never dreamed of. A casual comment about a birdsong might launch me into a delicious, bewildering morass of conjecture about instinct versus acquired learning and whether there is such a thing as true individual creativity. At first wide-eyed, I soon learned to participate in the vigorous debates.

Although both the girls had a similar effect on us Myers kids, the twins differed greatly from one another. Betty — slender, attractive, practical — was the active one but nevertheless a most enthusiastic visitor and ever sensitive to the feelings of others. She planned the parties, drove the car and boat, coaxed the outboard motor to top performance, and, like her mother, kept the excitement going for whatever we did. Dort — fair-skinned, rosy, dreamy — enjoyed athletic games, often played the piano, and played hymns for our island Sunday school when the service was held at their home.

When he was with them on the island, their tall, solemn father with his craggy features and shock of center-parted white hair gave dignity and authority to the service. The measured cadence of his deep voice with just a faint hint of a lisp commanded our attention. He often did not spend the summers with us, though, because he was needed on the Lafayette College campus in Easton, Pennsylvania, where he taught religion.

This left Mrs. Harris in charge, and she liked action. When there was nothing stirring on the island, she would start a rumor, then rush in to smooth things over when it reached a boil. Clothing found in the cottage was enough to fuel hints of strange parties. Gossip and outrage ran high. She might remark about the outcome of a tennis tournament or comment on a salad provided for a potluck — anything that could be variously interpreted or attributed to several people served the purpose. Far from harboring any meanness, she throve on reaching out to shy people — adults and youngsters alike — and was said to be famous for the mixers she initiated at the college.

One evening, one of so many happy times on their porch, stands out. It was the summer of 1928. But first a little background. During my junior year of high school, I had met Don Douglas in the church choir. He was a sophomore at the University of Minnesota, and his attentions were impressive, especially his invitation to a church dance and later to the military ball. It turned out that he roomed near my home and watched for me as I walked back from school late one afternoon.

"Well, hi. Do you live in this neck of the woods?" he asked innocently, as if his meeting me were pure accident. I did not realize that he stood six feet, six inches tall, for his muscular build disguised his height. His regular features, fair skin, and rugged coloring were set off by a mass of brown hair. He had the inevitable nickname: Curly. We visited easily as he accompanied me home. Because it was already time for dinner, I did not linger long. He asked if I would go to the First Congregational Church dinner dance with him. As I happily accepted, I stood a step above him and looked directly into his deep blue eyes. I had a feeling that I would always be able to count on this young man.

I was barely in time to help Mother get the food onto the table. As we sat down, I told the family about my exciting invitation, and they all rejoiced with me. Mother asked his name, and I realized he had said only Don; we had to consult the church choir directory to discover his last name.

I met Don Douglas in the church choir
during my junior year of high school.

Everyone teased me about agreeing to go out with a man
whose last name I didn't even know.

Don had never visited me at the island, but he was a
determined person. One evening he found his way to Zumbra Heights and hitched a ride across to the island. Mother,
who approved of Don, told him I was next door and as-

sured him he would be welcome. She directed him to the path along the fence that led to the Harrises' back gate. By this time it was dusk, and he must have been surprised not to see any lights burning as he approached the house.

Mrs. Harris had been holding forth in her favorite chair with a basket of sewing in her lap. Betty had started telling a mystery story in which the characters were stumbling about in an echoing cave with water seeping under their feet. Abruptly she called on Ev to continue the narrative. He introduced bats and a snake, which he knew she hated even to talk about, and Betty slipped into the kitchen for a glass of water. Returning to her place on the swinging bed where Ev was lying, she dropped a small chunk of ice inside his shirt. Wasting no time, he grabbed a thimble from the table and flipped a few drops of water at her.

"Wait, wait!" cried Mrs. Harris. "If you're going to have a water fight, put the pillows away first!"

We did. The boys followed Ev to the kitchen for supplies while Dort and I gave our allegiance to Betty. In and out, up and down we rampaged, dousing each other as we passed. Bob blew out the Rochester lamp when I was on the dark stairway alone. I couldn't hear anything. Feeling my way back to the kitchen, I joined the twins. The boys had vanished. We had been squirting spray bottles used to dampen clothes for ironing, but now we felt threatened. The boys must be hatching a plot to rush us. Helping me climb onto the wide mantel, Dort hid behind a bench, and Betty, ever the action girl, filled a small bucket and became our frontline troops.

Suddenly, instead of the sneak attack we expected, there was a decorous knock — to throw us off guard, no doubt. We would not be fooled! Betty snatched open the door and, keeping her body behind it, shot the water into the darkness.

Don, in white "ice cream" pants and navy blue jacket, stood shocked, dripping, and furious. Even dripping, he looked so dressed up and handsome. What a greeting we had given him! Ignominiously perched on the mantel in this silly kid game, I felt shy and apologetic. Our eyes met. He barely hesitated, then came over to help me down as I made introductions, and we all tried to explain why we were tossing water out the door. He used his cigarette lighter to light the kerosene lamp while Betty fetched a towel to dab at his clothes. We convinced him that we had been under siege and that there was nothing personal in our greeting him with a bucket of cold water.

Don was a favorite with my brothers, and soon the boys had crowded back into the porch. Mrs. Harris had made her stout self comfortable in a chair facing the lake. She rose as Don came in and, pushing her reddish-brown hair back from her flushed face with a plump hand, graciously offered him a chair. Like hers, it was low-slung, with a cushion supported by slender curved bands of metal. Don, a football player who weighed a bit over two hundred pounds, protested that the chair would never hold him. Mrs. Harris insisted, and when he continued to demur, she shoved him vigorously. Surprised and caught off balance, he sat down hard. The chair sagged. In a vigorous manner that suggested scrimmage practice, he scrambled to get his long legs under him, but the chair gave up entirely and dumped him onto the floor.

Don extricated himself and stood to view the wreckage.

Mrs. Harris began to giggle. Soon Don's hearty laughter joined in.

If ever a swain was tested, it was Don.

The Real World

AFTER DAD'S LATER THAN usual departure for Europe in 1928, when we sat down to our first supper without him, Mother asked the Lord's blessing on our food to keep us strong to do His will. She also asked Him to keep us safe in His care. We all knew she was thinking ahead to Dad's return and picturing her family happy and well, herself the good and faithful servant.

Mother was concerned about Bob's first job, which he had started that summer. He worked for the Minneapolis telephone company. He needed to allow a whole hour first to row across from the island to Zumbra, where he had obtained permission to park Dad's six-cylinder Nash Ambassador as well as his own newly acquired Indian motorcycle. We were all proud of him — especially Mother, who was not yet a driver — and of the confidence his employers already placed in him. Secretly, I saw driving as a great challenge — would I in my turn have the courage to learn to drive? I was sure I could never do it as well and as confidently as my brother did.

Mother also worried about my keeping company with Don, especially since he was four years older than I and had much more dating experience. I thought her uneasiness was overblown. In fact, he was so busy this summer helping on his father's farm that he didn't visit again and didn't have time to write often. He hoped to return to the university in the fall and was saving his wages. He confided that he had arranged to rent a room across Oak Street from us, so it was plain that he hoped to see more of me. (As things worked out, Everett saw more of Don than I did for a while. He and Don both followed the fire trucks when they came thundering up Oak Street, and it was not long before my brother was regularly joining Don in the little roadster he acquired.) I was sure there was no reason for her distress, but Mother never was one to let a problem develop because she had been negligent.

Mother and I got to know each other in a delightful way that summer. At times it was almost as if there were no difference in our ages. One day when we had filled the little kitchen with the rich aroma of baking bread, she joined the boys and me in stealing crusts from the loaves while they were still hot and crunchy. We crowned them with butter, which melted and slithered over our tongues. She talked of growing up in a minister's family with seven children and moving every four years, according to church policy. The food had to be stretched and clothing carefully mended and passed down, for the "preacher's kids" always had to look presentable.

She described the day of our long-ago arrival in Minneapolis in a dreary rain. Caring for three active children, all under six, had worn her down to ninety-six pounds; she was far from her family home in Evanston, Illinois, and now she was leaving behind the friendly college town of Oxford, Ohio.

This reminded me of a story Dad once recounted about a social rebuff soon after our arrival in Minneapolis. Mother had dressed up and dressed us little ones in our best to make a call on the older, childless wife of the head of the German department at the university. Not knowing that here in Minnesota the custom was to make these formal calls without children, she had thought her darlings would be admired and enjoyed. Conversation was chilly and stilted, and Mother was glad to escape after half an hour.

I tried to imagine how the incident might have seemed to the hostess. Did she worry about children tracking dirt onto her fine Persian carpet? Did she debate about offering tea or coffee for fear it might be spilled — or a precious cup broken? Had Mother thought ahead to bring a toy or book to keep Bob and me busy while she held Everett and made conversation? Mother's expectations had been based on memories of her own mother, who, as a Methodist minister's wife, had received callers for hours at a time and made them feel welcome.

Once Mother told a hilarious story of going on a picnic with an old beau on a bicycle built for two. Even after all these years, she was indignant as she described his pedaling faster and faster. He paid no attention to her warnings. When they flew down a long hill, she braked furiously until she saw that he was merrily dangling his feet off the pedals. She gave up then and watched their pop bottles swinging from the handlebars. When he finally braked, the bottles crashed together and shattered. Their spirits were dampened, and their lunch was decidedly dry.

Mother returned to the subject of Don, and I realized I did not want to discuss him anymore. She made sure I knew that she and Dad did not want me to go steady with anyone during my senior year of high school, but instead to make many new friends, both boys and girls. I listened dutifully but felt faintly resentful. I thought I knew Don better than she did. I had been grateful for her comments about my first proposal, but with Don it was different. Don would never be irresponsible, I was sure, but I began to see how many years it would be before I could undertake a commitment.

Sometimes in the evenings Mother sat at the piano, singing in her rich alto while Bob plucked chords on his banjo, Ev tootled on his clarinet, and I tried to keep up on a fat old-fashioned mandolin the Mudgetts lent me. We missed Dad, but I felt I knew Mother better than I ever had. She was quiet but steady as a rock, unchanged, only revealed, by Dad's absence.

About two weeks before Dad was to return, Bob came home one rainy night much later than usual. He woke Mother—as he had promised always to do—to say the car had stopped.

"I left it near the road to Excelsior. I'll have to go back in the morning to get it."

"But how did you get home?" Her voice was fuzzy with sleep.

"Hitchhiked and walked. I'm kind of wet, Mom. Got to get to bed."

He went upstairs.

The morning was clear and cloudless although the lawn showed evidence of heavy rain. Bob was up promptly but had little to say at breakfast. He took Everett with him on the motorcycle to go back for the car. It was right side up on an outside curve of the ditch, but it had rolled completely over.

A burned, blackened wreck, it lay in the roadside rubble. Just seeing it there was a traumatic experience for both boys, they told me later. Ev's eyes filled with tears as he looked at the blistered green paint he had helped his father wax. The top was torn and partly burned away; the crooked wheels, one of them broken, were half hidden in the weeds. Even Bob, who thought he knew what to expect, was not prepared for the dismal appearance of his father's beloved car in daylight. He stood silent and grim. His voice seemed to come from far away as he began to explain to Ev.

"I wasn't going fast, but it was raining hard. The car started skidding on that curve and just kept sliding whether I used the brakes or not. As I went down off the shoulder, it hit something and rolled."

Bob and the car had gone clear over. All the doors were jammed shut, and he was trapped.

"How did you get out?" Ev asked.

"See that black hole in the roof?" Bob said. "That's where a fence post punched through the top of the car as it rolled, not three inches from my head, I figure."

"But it could have killed you!"

"I guess."

"But you got out! How?"

"Look, Ev, car roofs are just made of chicken wire, wood slats, rubberized fabric, and cotton batting. I had to get out of there."

"Gosh, yes! The fire! You're not burned, are you?"

"No, I knew it was dangerous, but I was scared. I just tore at the roof and pushed until it gave way."

Bob and Ev climbed into the ditch and examined the burned wreck.

"Did you see the fire start, Bob?"

Bob hesitated. "Yes — well, yes. My paycheck was lying on the seat in my billfold, so I crawled back in to get it."

"Crawled back? When it was burning?"

"No, I knew it was dangerous, but I wasn't going to lose that check after all the work I'd done. The fire extinguisher was jammed. I couldn't loosen it."

"Did the fire department come? How did they know?"

A traveling salesman in the car behind Bob had seen him skid on the slick road. He took Bob to Excelsior to call a fire truck, but a neighbor had already phoned. The truck was on the way. When they met on the road, the salesman turned around and passed the truck to lead the way to the car. One of the firemen yelled to the salesman that it was a violation of the law to pass a fire truck; the salesman got so nervous he ran off the road, too. Another man pulled them out of the ditch and, after the fire was quenched, drove Bob to Zumbra.

In spite of what he had been through the night before, Bob still had some presence of mind.

"Mother doesn't need to know all the details," he told Ev, "but I'll have to tell her the facts because of the insurance papers."

When the boys came back across the lake, I was sitting with Mother on the front porch on the big bed where she and Dad slept. I knew as soon as I saw them that something was very wrong. Poor Bob didn't know how to soften the blow for Mother. I suppose there really wasn't any way. He left out the fence post that just missed his head, but he told us that the car rolled over and burned. I was speechless. What would I have done, had it happened to me? I would never have the courage to drive after this.

As Mother listened, her eyes widened, and she seemed to stop breathing. When she realized the danger Bob had been in and understood that the car was totally destroyed, she lay back on the bed and covered her face with her hands. Tears rolled out under her glasses and down her cheeks. I watched a wet spot grow and darken the old blue spread where it covered the pillow. I could hear my heart pounding. I didn't know what to say or do. I saw her lips move, and I thought I heard her say "Oh, Walter!"

Never before had I seen my mother cry. Tiny as she was, she seemed to shrink before my eyes. We children stood awkwardly silent, overwhelmed by what was and what might have been. Finally I leaned over to touch her shoulder. She reached up and held onto my hand. Her tears increased, but only for a few moments. Then she sat up, wiped her face, and cleaned her glasses. Practical as always, she hurried us to the kitchen to wash up for lunch.

We rejoiced at Dad's return; his health was apparently quite restored, and he took the accident in stride. "Everyone seems to need one wake-up call," he comforted. "I have confidence there won't be another. We can't live our lives just trying to avoid accidents. Accidents happen. Face it. Adjust. And go on."

My Friend the Loon

IN LATE AUGUST before my senior year of high school, the complexity of schedules and school was almost upon us, but Mother had one more event on her mind. She had invited guests from the city for our next-to-the-last weekend on the island. On a glorious Saturday morning she asked me to go to the mainland to mail a letter outlining final arrangements for her friends while she readied the upstairs dormitory. Dad was already harvesting in the garden, and the boys were off somewhere with pals of Bob's. Remembering the gravel road leading over the hill to the mailbox, I added tennis shoes to my costume of navy gym bloomers and a white blouse with a red scarf at the neck.

I was delighted with my assignment, for there was no place I would rather be than out on the ever-bewitching water. I flew down the steeply sloping yard and the stairs to the lake almost faster than my feet could keep up. Flipping the canoe right side up, I pushed off.

I was on the lake! It mattered not one whit that without ballast the prow jutted high out of the water, and the uncertain breeze caught it like a sail from time to time, making my progress erratic. The breeze also teased the waters into sparkly ripples, and the bay enticed me into its huge expanse. Not a boat was in sight all the way to the White Bridge, nor was any to be seen to the east, where I now pointed the canoe. I had the world to myself as I paddled between Eagle Island and Gallagher's Point and crossed Zumbra Bay. I finished the familiar trip and pulled my canoe up on shore. Soon I was climbing Zumbra Hill. As I descended the far side to Highway 7, a rabbit hopped lazily away under the cedars. I tucked the letter into the Crane Island box, raised the red metal flag, and watched a lone pickup truck disappear down the otherwise empty highway.

Back in the canoe, I continued to feel heady. The deep blue sky of late summer was without even a whisker of cloud. My paddle dimpled the water, the pattern quickly erased by tiny waves. As I looked back, the slight triangular wake of the boat was smoothed as if it had never been. I felt an urge to blend into all this beauty, to abandon the canoe and slide into the water.

Instead, as I rounded Gallagher's Point, I watched a single crane, silent and aloof, soar overhead and disappear into the treetops of Wawatasso. It would soon be time for the big birds to move south. By then we Myerses would have returned to the city. My mind slipped away from that path. Here on Crane Island I was in a magic bubble that sheltered me from problems. The world out there would in time lead to adventures, I was sure, some spiced with excitement and danger, but I was content to let all that wait. Everything was so perfect right now.

Suddenly I was surprised to hear the penetrating, warbling call of a loon, and then answering laughter from another and another. Three loons with drifts of tiny white spots across their shiny black backs rode high on the water near the point of Eagle Island. I noiselessly paddled near. They moved away without apparent alarm. I stayed close. One by one they dived. First the head with its big flat bill bent low and slipped under the water, then the long, snake-like neck. The body followed as smoothly as if it had been turned to shiny liquid and poured into the lake. There was no stirring of the surface, nothing to indicate where they were. I waited and almost gave up before they reappeared far out in the lake. Still intrigued, I approached silently and again observed their sinuous dive. This time one reappeared near me. The other two I later glimpsed far off, almost to Wawatasso, still swimming away.

I paddled gently toward the loon, who let me approach within a few yards before he made an effortless dive. I moved toward where I thought he would surface, but he reappeared soundlessly in the opposite direction, then swam a little way toward me. What was this? A friendly gesture? But no, as soon as I turned my craft toward the loon, he dived again. Now he sneaked under the canoe to surprise me by coming up nearby on the other side. Knowing that loons have keen underwater vision to find food and elude enemies, I was sure this sport was not accidental. Apparently the loon was enjoying this game as much as I was.

Trying to do the impossible and outguess him, I once positioned the canoe only a couple of boat lengths from where he surfaced with a strange, unearthly cry. Perhaps he was laughing at me. He was certainly leading me on; we must have played for over half an hour before he abruptly wearied of the amusement and faced away toward the long stretch of empty bay.

Spellbound, I watched as this creature so incredibly skillful in the water clumsily tried to elevate his plump body with violent fanning of his wings. His feet splashed desperate footsteps halfway across the bay before he was completely airborne. The loon had mastered his awkwardness and become almost as adept in the sky as in the water. I marveled at his metamorphosis and then his rapid flight off and away into the distance.

The loon and I had worked our way almost to Crane Island, so now I was near home. Our kingfisher flashed a flurry of blue and white as he took his accustomed place on the wire of the water trolley. I guided my canoe to shore and found my parents reading on the front porch.

"I s'pose Ruth is back from Battle Lake by now," I ventured.

"Oh, yes, I'm sure," Mother answered. "And didn't Anne's letter say they were closing their St. Croix cabin last week?"

"What day will we be leaving, Mom? I don't want to miss starting day at U High. All of a sudden I can't wait."

Mother looked up at me quizzically. "What's happened to you? I thought you couldn't bear to leave."

"I don't know. I guess I sort of said good-bye out there — good-bye to the lake for this year, anyway. And there was

Canoes were my wings.

a little loon . . . " I barely whispered, "He tried so hard, but then he broke free and soared off and away."

"A loon?" Dad must have heard a yearning in my voice. "A loon? Then that's why you kept maneuvering the canoe so skillfully around the bay, Miggles. It seems like yesterday that I was teaching you to hold a paddle."

Mother smiled indulgently. "Well, you managed to get my letter mailed, I hope."

Afterword

MY SENIOR YEAR of high school was wonderful; it brought lasting friendships and scholastic and athletic honors as well as Don's love, which ripened during our college years. Without apparent jealousy, he tolerated my dating others, two of whom became very dear to me, but he was always my chosen partner for sorority parties. By the end of my sophomore year at the University of Minnesota, the realities of the Depression had made me relinquish my dreams of writing and settle on a five-year course in medical social work. My mentor arranged a position for me at Columbia-Presbyterian Medical Center in New York City, where I had to make a minimum commitment of two years. I felt it was unfair to both Don and me to be formally engaged; he assured me, though, that if I did not marry him, he would never marry. The cards that accompanied flowers and gifts continued to say "Always, Don."

Meanwhile, he finished college in engineering-business and, finding the job market grim, formed a partnership in a small printing business. His partner absconded, leaving him with several thousand dollars of debt, which he slaved to repay. Then he took a job with the Federal Land Banks. When that work proved to involve mainly foreclosing on capable farmers who were victims of hard times, he quit and finally found rewarding work with the new Soil Conservation Service. There his farm background gave him valuable insight into farmers' attitudes and needs, and his solid values and genial personality quickly won their confidence.

After two and a half years of the heady excitement of New York City, I returned to the Twin Cities to set up a medical social service department at Gillette State Hospital for Crippled Children in St. Paul.

A year after our wedding in June 1937 in my parents' home and a trip to the Black Hills and Glacier Park, Don and I had a second honeymoon in the little cottage on Crane Island. We let all the clocks and watches run down and stop. We drifted as far from our busy routines as we could. If it pleased our fancy, we had a dip before breakfast, or we went canoeing in the moonlight or skinny dipping after dark. We felt again the magic of going barefoot on Crane Island.

Then one day fifty years, three children, and seven grandchildren later, Don took my left hand and gazed at the small diamond in my engagement ring.

"Wouldn't you like an eternity ring now? One of those with diamonds all around?"

I hesitated only a moment. "No," I answered. "No, I like the one I have. Besides, you could never again afford to pay what you did for this one." He stiffened in surprise, and I added, "I've never known what you paid for my ring, but I know it cost everything you had in the world. This is the one I will always treasure."

The look in his eyes was worth more to me than any number of diamonds. Two years after the celebration of our fiftieth wedding anniversary Don died.

The "Myers" cottage is still owned by the woman to whom Dad sold it in 1954. Mother had died in 1952, and Dad remarried two years later and moved east. At that time none of us children was in a position to use it; Don and I were living on his family's farm and tending the year's first hay crop when the dock needed to be put in and yard care started. Everett and his family lived in Independence, Missouri, where he used his mechanical genius at Lake City Arsenal. Bob had set his engineering skills aside temporarily while he earned a master's degree in social welfare; he moved his family to Williamsburg, Massachusetts, where he headed and vastly expanded a family agency and worked with Smith College in Northampton in training students.

Superdad and Mother are gone, along with the Eustises and the Edholms and many of the others. Second- and third-generation Harrises, Brandts, and Amys (McKendrys) now vacation on Crane Island.

My recent trips to the island with Ted and Doni Greer and later with the Tim Munkebys (whose fast boats shrank the miles) were like trips back in time — the cottages and yards look much the same as they did in the days of "little

Minnehaha," and there are only three new ones — but there are differences, too. Crane Island is now used more as a weekend retreat than for summer-long occupancy. Telephones have been added — and electricity, so ice delivery is no longer necessary. Noisy boats threaten the safety and pleasure of swimmers.

A big Hennepin County park opened May 1997 at Lake Minnetonka Regional Park on the nearby shore off County Road 44 and contributed to the lake traffic. A museum, a half-acre swimming area, fishing and boat docks, and a parking lot are planned.

Tiny Crane Island survives as a refreshing taste of the past in a sea of change.